TRACING YOUR
CANAL ANCESTORS

FAMILY HISTORY FROM PEN & SWORD BOOKS

TRACING YOUR CANAL ANCESTORS

A Guide for Family Historians

SUE WILKES

Pen & Sword
FAMILY HISTORY

First published in Great Britain in 2011 by
PEN AND SWORD FAMILY HISTORY
an imprint of
Pen & Sword Books Ltd
47 Church Street
Barnsley
South Yorkshire
S70 2AS

ISBN 978 1 84884 238 0

A CIP catalogue record for this book is
available from the British Library

Typeset in 10pt Palatino by Mac Style, Beverley, East Yorkshire
Printed and bound in the UK by CPI

Pen & Sword Books Ltd incorporates the Imprints of Pen & Sword
Aviation, Pen & Sword Family History, Pen & Sword Maritime, Pen
& Sword Military, Pen & Sword Discovery, Wharncliffe Local History,
Wharncliffe True Crime, Wharncliffe Transport, Pen & Sword Select,
Pen & Sword Military Classics, Leo Cooper, The Praetorian Press,
Remember When, Seaforth Publishing and Frontline Publishing.

For a complete list of Pen & Sword titles please contact
PEN & SWORD BOOKS LIMITED
47 Church Street, Barnsley, South Yorkshire, S70 2AS, England
E-mail: enquiries@pen-and-sword.co.uk
Website: www.pen-and-sword.co.uk

CONTENTS

For Nigel, Lizzie and Gareth

ACKNOWLEDGEMENTS

Many people have helped to create this book. It would not have been possible without the help and support of my husband Nigel, and my children Elizabeth and Gareth.

I owe special thanks to Ian Wilkes for sharing with me his research into the Wilkes family tree. I am also very grateful to Kenneth and Lily Wakefield for reliving their childhoods growing up on the inland waterways, and to Janet Lane for granting permission to include her childhood memories. Brenda Ward, editor of the *Boundary Post* journal, has also been incredibly helpful.

I would also like to thank waterways archivists Linda Barley at Ellesmere Port and Caroline Jones at Gloucester Docks for all their help and patience with my queries. Authors Joseph Boughey, Mike Clarke and Basil Jeuda have also lent their assistance.

I am very grateful to Mike Eddison at Cheshire Archives and Local Studies for giving permission to reproduce and quote from original documents, and staff at Cheshire libraries for their help. I would also like to thank the many archivists and librarians in Britain who have helped with my queries. Any mistakes in the text are my own.

Thank you to Fiona Carding and the Black Country Living Museum for kind permission to include a photograph of their historic canal-side area.

Crown copyright material from TNA website is reproduced by permission of The National Archives. Information from the PRONI online catalogue is quoted by permission of the Deputy Keeper of the Records, Public Record Office of Northern Ireland. The National Archives of Scotland have also given permission to quote from their website.

Records held by Cheshire Archives and Local Studies Service are reproduced with kind permission of Cheshire Shared Services to whom copyright is reserved.

Every effort has been made to trace copyright holders for images used in this work. The publishers welcome information on any attributions that have been omitted.

Please note that where the term 'bargee' is used in the text in relation to narrow boatmen, it is a direct quote and must be seen in its contemporary context.

Last but not least, I would like to thank Simon Fowler and Rupert Harding of Pen & Sword Books for their help and encouragement.

LIST OF ILLUSTRATIONS

All engravings from the author's collection and the Nigel Wilkes collection. All photos © Sue and Nigel Wilkes.

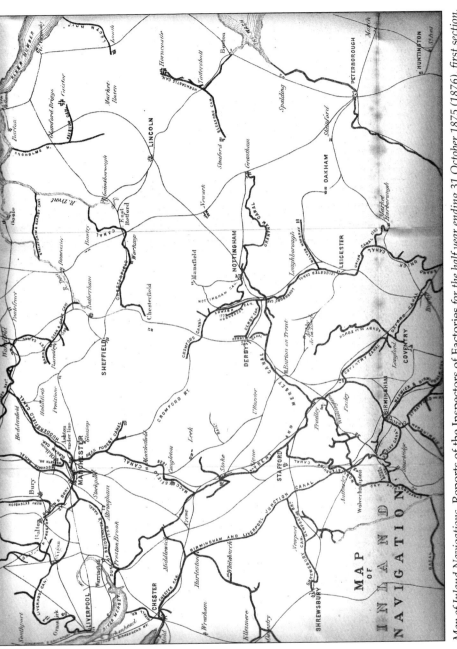

Map of Inland Navigations. Reports of the Inspectors of Factories for the half year ending 31 October 1875 (1876), first section.

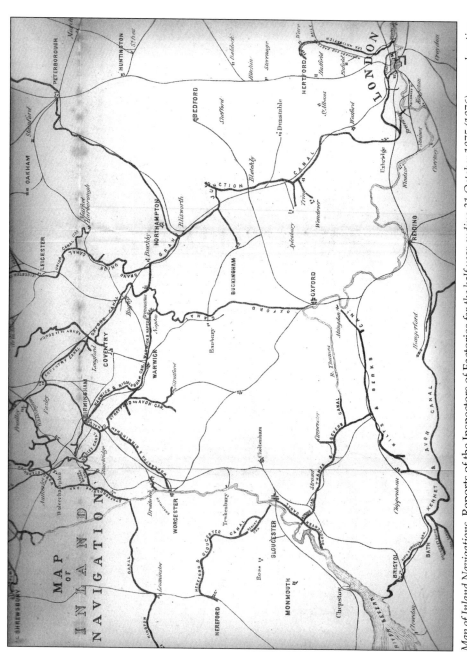

Map of Inland Navigations. Reports of the Inspectors of Factories *for the half year ending 31 October 1875 (1876), second section.*

Chapter 1

THE CANAL PIONEERS

The story of Britain's inland waterways is also the story of the thousands of families who depended on them for a living. Engineers designed the canals, sturdy navvies carved them out of the landscape, and men, women and children worked on the boats and kept the wheels of industry running smoothly.

If you walk along a canal towpath today, the water is busy with passing pleasure craft. But the canals were once the lifeblood of Britain's industry, and many people once lived and worked here.

Walk a little further, and you may find some clues to a long-vanished past: a lock keeper's cottage, or a lengthsman's hut. Boarded up, windowless warehouses stand empty and neglected. The docks and wharves, which once rang with boatmen's shouts and the clatter of boats being loaded and unloaded, are silent now. Most canal craft are now pleasure boats or floating homes, although a few working boats still ply their trade.

The aim of this book is to help people with an ancestor who worked on the canals, or for a canal company, to explore their family history further. The book is in two parts. The first part explores the story of Britain's canal carrying trade and the social history of its workers. Examples are given of useful documentary evidence and sources where appropriate.

The second part explains how to take your research further. Basic family history guidance is included for those readers completely new to genealogy, but this section can be skipped by seasoned campaigners. Many different sources are explored such as census records, parliamentary papers and other publications. There are tips on how to find health (canal-boat) registers and other documents related to canal life mentioned in the social history chapters. Examples are given of some possible pitfalls you may encounter while conducting your search.

There are directories of the main archives and repositories with canal-related materials, sections on 'family history help' with online resources where you can search databases of canal-boat ancestors, and a guide to waterways museums where you can see how your ancestors lived and worked.

Although the book largely concentrates on England and Wales (the centre of the inland waterways network), some brief pointers on researching canal ancestors in Scotland and Ireland are included. Canals in countries outside Britain are beyond the scope of this work.

This island nation had long been accustomed to move bulky goods by water whenever possible because the highways were so atrocious. Roads were little better than rough tracks in some places and almost impassable during the winter months or after heavy rain. Eighteenth-century travellers like Arthur Young found turnpike roads in Lancashire which had ruts 4ft deep that filled with mud after a wet summer.

Carrying goods over land was incredibly expensive except for short distances. In the 1750s it cost about £7 to send 1 ton of goods from Birmingham to London, and £13 from Leeds to London. Trains of pack horses were the most common mode of transport, so quantities were limited to the amount a horse could manage on its back. If a half-decent road was available, waggons pulled by horses or oxen were pressed into service for carrying freight, but these roads were few and far between.

Rivers were the obvious solution to the problem of moving goods easily over long distances. The rivers Severn and Thames were busy trade routes. But many rivers had all kinds of navigational hazards associated with them such as fishing weirs. Mill owners, too, took water from rivers to power their waterwheels. Tidal stretches of rivers could be extremely dangerous for shipping, in addition to delays caused by waiting for the right tide.

Over time, the navigation on rivers was improved. Deeper channels were dredged and weeds cut back on the river bed and banks. In some areas 'flash-locks' were introduced to ensure boats had an easier passage on rivers that had sudden changes in the height of the river bed. These precursors of the modern-style locks on canals, in effect, stored water until required. Then a lock gate was opened and the waiting boats went through with a 'flash' or flush of water to help speed their journey.

The first 'pound' locks in Britain, constructed with a gate at each end, were built on the Exeter Canal (completed in 1566). This 3-mile ship canal was cut to avoid a huge weir built by great landowners across the River Exe to power their mills which effectively closed the river to sea-going vessels.

Little capital was available for major engineering projects, but a few attempts were made to give ships an easier passage along rivers. The Wey Navigation made the river navigable from the Thames at Weybridge to Guildford; it was completed in 1653. Fifteen years later, work began on improving the navigation of the rivers Aire and Calder in Yorkshire in 1699, and this waterway gave a huge boost to the county's industry. During 1720–1721, Acts of Parliament were passed to improve the rivers Mersey, Irwell, Weaver and Douglas in north-west England.

The Newry Canal in Ireland was probably the first completely artificial waterway (with a summit level fed by a reservoir) in Britain. The canal, which joined the port of Newry with Lough Neagh and was opened to traffic in 1742, gave Dublin merchants greater access to collieries in Tyrone. Lancashire-born Thomas Steers (1672–1750) was one of the engineers involved in its construction.

In England, the next significant development in the story of canals was the Sankey Navigation. Industries in Liverpool and the salt-producing

The railway viaduct of the recently opened Liverpool and Manchester Railway (in the background) spans the Sankey Canal (Brook). Unknown artist, Penny Magazine, *30 April 1833.*

towns of Cheshire were hungry for coal. In 1755 Parliament granted permission for the Sankey Brook to be made navigable from the Mersey (about 2 miles below Warrington) to St Helens. When the engineer in charge, Henry Berry, found the original plan was unworkable, he simply cut a canal instead and used the brook as a feeder supply. The canal first opened two years later.

Contemporaries regarded Francis Egerton, 3rd Duke of Bridgewater (1736–1803) as the true pioneer of the canal system in Britain. The 'Canal Duke' proved it was faster and, most importantly, more profitable to transport coal by canal than over land.

The Duke, in common with other noblemen of his day, enjoyed a tour of the Continent when he was a young man. He was greatly impressed by the magnificent Canal du Midi at Languedoc in the south of France. Britain lagged behind its rivals on the Continent, where for many years goods haulage by water was far more technically advanced than in Britain.

The Egertons owned collieries at Worsley. For some time the family had wanted a cheaper way to transport its coal to Manchester, where there were many willing customers for fuel. The Duke, no doubt inspired by the wonders he had seen on his travels and by the recently opened Sankey Navigation nearby, decided a canal was the way forward.

Initially, the Duke and his land agent John Gilbert proposed a modest scheme: a short canal from the Worsley mines to Hollin Ferry on the Mersey and Irwell Navigation. After opposition from the Mersey and Irwell Navigation Co., which wanted to keep its monopoly on carrying in the area, the Duke and Gilbert determined to get Bridgewater coal sent to Manchester by as direct a route as possible.

They faced a major technical problem: how to cross the Irwell valley. It was probably Gilbert who came up with the solution: the Bridgewater Canal would soar across the River Irwell via a mighty aqueduct. The Duke and Gilbert appointed a brilliant millwright, James Brindley (1716–1772), to put their vision into practice. When the first boat sailed over Barton Aqueduct on 17 July 1761, nothing like it had ever been seen before in Britain. It was one of the wonders of the age.

The new canal halved the price of coal in Manchester to 3½d per cwt. A few years later, the Bridgewater Canal was extended to the Mersey at Runcorn (so boats could now reach the port of Liverpool).

The Duke's canal was a leap of faith in financial as well as engineering terms. According to Brindley's biographer Samuel Smiles, the Duke got

The young Duke of Bridgewater pictured with Barton Aqueduct behind him. Unknown artist, Lives of the Engineers: Brindley and the Early Engineers *(John Murray, 1874).*

into a huge amount of debt: it cost the princely sum of £200,000 to build the canal from Worsley to Manchester and link it to Runcorn.

But the canal was a huge financial success: it eventually yielded a profit of £80,000 per annum. While it was under construction, another important canal scheme was mooted.

Josiah Wedgwood (1730–1795), the 'father' of the Staffordshire potteries, wanted to expand his business at Burslem, but was hampered by the poor roads in the area. The costs of transporting the raw materials he needed, such as china clay, were prohibitive. His beautiful 'cream ware' had to be carried by packhorse and was often smashed to pieces by the time it arrived.

Wedgwood and others wanted a canal to link the rivers Severn and Trent: the 'Grand Trunk'. The Duke of Bridgewater, foreseeing the

Etruscan Bone and Flint Mill (Jesse Shirley's) on the Trent & Mersey Canal at Etruria. Shirley supplied Josiah Wedgwood with bone ash for the production of his world-renowned china.

possibility of higher profits if the new canal linked with his, threw his weight behind the scheme.

Brindley and others hoped the Grand Trunk Canal would be the first step in creating a canal network called 'The Cross'. The Grand Trunk would form the 'spine' of England's waterways. When more canals linked to it from the south-west and south-east (forming a 'cross' or 'X' across England) manufacturers in the Midlands would have access to the rivers Thames and Severn.

Wedgwood helped push the Grand Trunk scheme through and invested thousands of pounds of his own capital in it. It was only fitting that he cut the first sod of the canal on 26 July 1766. He built a new pottery and a handsome new house at Etruria by the canal. When the main line of the Grand Trunk (later known as the Trent & Mersey) was completed in 1777, Wedgwood's wares could be loaded straight into canal boats.

However, lack of funding and other difficulties meant that Brindley's 'Cross' was not achieved until 1790 when the Oxford Canal and Coventry Canal were fully open.

By the early 1800s Brindley's Grand Trunk canal provided a thoroughfare from manufacturers' and merchants' own doorsteps to the 'principal sea-ports … of Bristol, Liverpool and Hull'. Before the canal's construction, the minerals of the counties along its route – 'ironstone, lead, copper, calamine, marble, limestone etc.' had 'lain undisturbed' because of the prohibitive cost of land carriage. Now the 'salt works at Northwich, and the manufactures of Nottingham, Leicester, and Derby' all benefited from the new route, and cargoes of 'corn, timber, wool, hides' found an 'easy and cheap conveyance'. (Cooke's *Topographical and Statistical Description of Staffordshire*, c.1803).

Brindley preferred to work with nature whenever possible to save costs. His 'contour canals' such as the Oxford Canal followed the curves of the landscape. As time went on, carriers found these meandering routes were too slow, and some of his cuts become obsolete or were 'straightened', as on the Birmingham Canal.

Some natural obstacles required innovative technical solutions and canal builders such as Brindley, Thomas Telford, John Smeaton and William Jessop created some amazing feats of engineering. The Ellesmere Canal (designed by Telford and Jessop) soared across the Dee valley on the breathtakingly beautiful Pontcysyllte Aqueduct, which took eight years to construct.

The breathtaking Pontcysyllte Aqueduct constructed by Thomas Telford and William Jessop to carry the Ellesmere Canal (now the Llangollen Canal) across the Dee valley. Unknown artist, Lives of the Engineers: History of Roads: Metcalfe, Telford *(John Murray, 1874).*

Joseph Hemingway noted in his *History of the City of Chester* (1831) that the trough carrying the canal was made from 'cast iron plates 20ft wide, 6ft deep, and 320ft long … supported by nineteen pair(s) of conical stone pillars at 52ft asunder, and the middle ones 125 feet in height'.

On the Leeds and Liverpool Canal, several sets of locks, including the impressive Bingley Five-Rise Lock, overcame a change in level of 120ft. When the stretch of canal (from Skipton to just below a junction with the Bradford Canal at Shipley) was opened in the spring of 1774, a gushing reporter from the *Scots Magazine* dubbed it: 'the noblest works of that kind … in the whole universe'.

Canal boats were ideal for moving weighty freight such as coal and limestone. A great variety of cargoes were carried: bricks, salt, pottery, china clay, stone, manure, timber and so on.

Some carriers handled extremely hazardous goods. On 28 September 1818 there was a massive explosion in a warehouse belonging to the Nottingham Canal Co. Here twenty-one barrels of gunpowder had been stored after being shipped from Gainsborough. One of the barrels leaked and left a trail of powder. A 'heedless boatman', Joseph Musson, thought he would create his own firework display and threw a hot cinder onto the powder.

The ensuing explosion was heard 10 miles away. The luckless Musson was blown 'a great distance' into some fields where he was found 'in several parts', and another seven men and two boys died in the blast (White's *History, Gazetteer of Nottingham*, 1832).

Canals were seen as a profitable investment, and 'canal mania' gripped the nation during the 1790s. People rushed to buy shares in the many canal schemes which were floated at this time. Two shares in the Leeds and Liverpool Canal were advertised in *The Times* (24 March 1794): 'The Canal [is] in the most prosperous state, and as rapidly increasing in value as any in the kingdom'.

The *New Monthly Museum* reported the grand opening of the Regent's Canal on 1 August 1820. The waterway linked 'all the principal canals in England with the River Thames'. The canal's managing committee, which included the famous architect John Nash and chief engineer James Morgan, marked the event with a voyage on the canal on 'one of the City's state barges, which had been borrowed for the occasion … accompanied by several other barges, having on board bands of music, and decorated with flags and streamers for the occasion'.

The 'Paddington barges' had a terrific race to see which one would be first to land a cargo at the canal basin. The winner was the '*William*, from which was landed the first produce and a cask of ale, which was immediately drank [*sic*] upon the spot by the navigators with loud huzzahs, to the prosperity of the undertaking'.

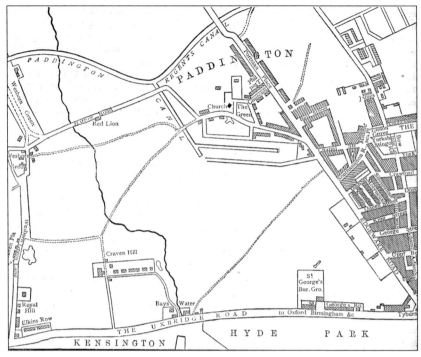

Map of Paddington showing the route of the Paddington and Regent's Canal. Old and New London, *Vol. V (Cassell, Petter & Galpin, c.1890).*

The canals brought immense benefits to Britain. They revolutionized transport, reduced freight costs and opened up new markets. They made possible cheaper supplies of coal and other materials needed for industry, which helped to fuel the Industrial Revolution. Canal boats brought staple foods like potatoes and flour to growing industrial towns such as Manchester.

In general, British canals were built by private enterprise. Public money was only rarely involved, as in the Royal Military Canal (begun in 1804) and the Caledonian Canal in Scotland (begun in 1804).

At the height of canal mania so many canal schemes were proposed that in 1792 Parliament decided canal plans must be deposited with the clerk of the peace for each county, and many of these plans can be found in local record offices. The most successful canals, like the Bridgewater and Grand Trunk, were those promoted by industry. Some proposals were purely speculative; they were ill-thought out and never materialized.

The birth of each canal followed a roughly similar process. First, the canal's promoters (manufacturers or landowners who hoped to make a profit) would engage an engineer such as Brindley or John Smeaton (1724–1792) to survey and plan out the line of the proposed waterway.

When a company wanted to build a canal, it could not just start digging a large hole wherever it wanted. In most cases an Act of Parliament was required before the company could set the navvies to work on the cut. Sometimes a canal proposal aroused great opposition and many petitions would be sent to Parliament against it.

Opponents included river navigation companies worried about the loss of freight, or fledgling companies who wanted to publicize the merits

---

Case Study

In 1818 the *Fifteenth Report of the Commissioners for Making and Maintaining the Caledonian Canal* was published by Parliament. The canal's construction was proving vastly more expensive than forecast by its engineer, Thomas Telford, and the waterway was only partially open. The report explained how the canal was progressing and detailed the physical obstacles being surmounted by Telford and his workforce. It itemised the timber and other materials required and the companies that supplied them, legal fees, transport costs, running expenses, etc. The report gave the names and salaries of the engineers and works supervisors responsible for overseeing the project, the lawyers involved, accountants and so on.

Thomas Telford was paid £4,099 4s for 'general superintendence and management' from 1803–1814. John Telford (no relation), the engineer in charge of the Corpach end of the canal, had earned £600 but died during the course of the work. His widow was paid a 'gratuity' of £50 to 'defray the cost' of the coach trip back to her home in Chester.

Boulton & Watt of Birmingham supplied three steam engines. Barges were needed for 'floating the Steam Engine Machines' which were needed to power the dredgers used to deepen Lochs Oich and Loch Doughfour. The names of individual navvies, carpenters and boatmen needed were not listed but there was a payment of £127 7s 0½d for 'whiskey allowed to men working in the water'.

of their own projects, or other canal companies worried they would lose business. Canal companies paid compensation to landowners affected by the scheme, but some estate owners just did not want their land cut up and would lobby Parliament to stop the plans. In these cases a parliamentary committee took detailed witness statements from engineers and other interested parties.

Similarly, when railways were constructed, canal companies sent petitions against the new 'iron roads' to Parliament. The House of Lords records in the Parliamentary Archives bear witness to these early transport wars (unfortunately many early House of Commons records on canals were destroyed by fire in 1834).

Parliamentary papers, committee reports and minutes of evidence often contain detailed statements from engineers such as James Brindley

'Neptune's Staircase'. Thomas Telford's impressive series of eight locks at Banavie on the Caledonian Canal. Mountain Moor and Loch Illustrated by Pen and Pencil (Sir Joseph Causton & Sons, 1894).

regarding the feasibility and construction of canals. Brindley famously told a House of Commons committee that he believed rivers had been created merely to 'feed navigable canals' (Dugdale's *New British Traveller*, 1819).

Some canal projects such as the Caledonian Canal were major public works undertaken with the dual purpose of providing employment as well as improving transport communications. Every penny of taxpayers' money spent had to be accounted for and the accounts were published in parliamentary papers. (See Section A1 for information on how to find parliamentary papers.)

Rival firms could sink a canal company's new venture during its planning stages. The Chester Canal, first authorized in 1772, aimed to connect Chester with the Grand Trunk Canal at Middlewich. But the Grand Trunk company and Duke of Bridgewater campaigned against it so successfully that the canal's construction was permitted only if it stopped 100yd away from the Grand Trunk. The canal terminated at Nantwich instead, and without a through link to the Midlands, it was a dead duck commercially. Over half a century passed before the section to the Trent & Mersey at Middlewich was authorized (1826) and Chester had its link to the potteries at last.

If all went well and an Act of Parliament was passed authorizing the canal, its promoters raised money by issuing shares (the Duke of Bridgewater's immense personal investment was exceptional). Once cutting the canal had commenced, if the company ran out of money (and canal building was an expensive business), it had to raise more money from its shareholders.

Landowners' intransigence caused real problems even after Parliament authorized canal works. When the Bridgewater Canal was extended to Runcorn, and the works hit difficulties, Sir Richard Brooke of Norton Priory refused to let the canal come anywhere near his property. The canal had an unfinished section through the Brooke estates across which goods had to be carried by cart until the Duke sweetened the pill with a hefty payment and Brooke sold him the necessary bit of land so the canal could be completed.

Meanwhile, the number of miles of inland waterways increased in other parts of Britain as part of the general improvements in navigation already under way. Work began on the Forth and Clyde Canal in 1768; Smeaton oversaw its construction.

The Grand Canal in Ireland was first authorized in 1772. The chief canals in South Wales (to serve the ironworks and collieries) were completed in the 1790s.

Some canals were extremely late coming to fruition. The Macclesfield Canal (after opposition from the Canal Duke) was not completed until 1831 and soon succumbed to railway competition. By the early 1820s there were over 4,000 miles of navigable waterways in Britain, and the most important routes were virtually complete by 1835.

Since the inland waterway network was built by many different (and competing) private companies, there was no 'joined-up thinking' to oversee its growth. In most cases a canal was built to serve local interests. There was no standard 'gauge' for canals and this resulted in a complex system with different canal widths, lock widths and hence boat sizes.

When Brindley planned his Grand Trunk (Trent & Mersey) Canal, he made a fateful decision. He decided to make the Harecastle Tunnel 12ft high and only 9ft wide. There was no towpath.

Canal engineer James Brindley (1716–1772). Lives of the Engineers: Brindley and the Early Engineers (*John Murray, 1874*).

Now the locks at Runcorn (where the Bridgewater Canal joined the Mersey) were constructed 72ft long and 15ft wide so that Mersey 'flats' (large flat-bottomed vessels) could negotiate them easily. If this lock size had been used as a 'template' for other canals, then it's possible a national 'wide gauge' waterways system might have been created.

Brindley's decision was almost certainly influenced by the cost and technical difficulties he had to overcome in cutting the 2,880yd-long tunnel (a hitherto unmatched engineering feat). The consequence of building a narrow tunnel was that there was no point wasting money on constructing wide locks elsewhere on the canal. The Grand Trunk locks were only wide enough to accommodate boats 7ft wide: the 'narrow boat' was born.

When another canal company wanted to link up with Brindley's 'narrow gauge' canal, by necessity, their canal boats had to fit within the framework he had created. Consequently the vast majority of the Midlands canals network could only take narrow boats. The amount of freight a narrow boat could carry was about 25 to 30 tons. This seemed adequate at the time, especially for short-distance haulage, but there were inherent problems in the system.

The lack of a 'standard gauge' meant carriers faced difficulties sending goods by canal over long distances. Goods had to be trans-shipped when moving from a 'wide' canal to a 'narrow' waterway. This disorganized evolution of the waterways sowed the seeds of its future decline and made it much harder for canal firms to compete with railways.

When the spectre of railway competition appeared, this size limitation on freight seemed antiquated. Efforts were made to do away with bottlenecks in the system such as the infamous Harecastle tunnel: Telford built another, wider tunnel very close to Brindley's original, and it opened in 1827.

The Canal Duke, Francis Egerton, died nearly thirty years before the birth of the first passenger railway. Samuel Smiles recorded that this far-sighted man had forebodings about the effect they might have on his business. 'We may do very well', he said to a friend, 'if we can keep clear of these ___ tram-roads'.

At first it seemed the Duke's premonition was incorrect. When the railway age dawned in 1830 with the opening of the Liverpool and Manchester Railway, people predicted the Bridgewater Canal would be killed off within a year and its water 'covered in rushes'. Yet over four decades later Smiles noted the Duke's canal 'continues to carry as much traffic as ever', although it had lost passenger traffic to the railway.

Tramroads or railways were not always direct competitors with canals in their early years. To save money, sometimes canal companies used a plateway (a type of railed road with waggons drawn by horses), tramroads or inclined planes to overcome differences in height along their route.

The Trent & Mersey built a tramroad from Froghall to Caldon Low in the late 1770s. According to the *British Cyclopaedia* (1838) the Monmouthshire Canal, on which work first began in 1792, was 'remarkable for the extent of its railways and inclined planes'.

The Cromford and High Peak Railway (first authorized in 1825) connected the Peak Forest Canal and Cromford Canal. The *Mechanics' Magazine* (1832) reported that this railway had several sections with inclined planes and 'stationary engines' were used 'to haul the carriages with passengers and goods up the inclined planes and let them down again'.

The railways did not devastate the canal carrying trade overnight. It was not until after 1840 that railway competition first began to bite. Even then, some canal companies expanded as smaller carriers left the waterways, and they were able to maintain a successful business.

After the opening of the London and Birmingham Railway in 1835, the Grand Junction Canal's tonnage increased over the next ten years from 310,475 to 480,626 tons.

The waterways were hampered by legal restrictions which reduced their competitiveness, however. For example, the toll system made canal freight more expensive than rail. Canal companies were not allowed to vary tolls until the Canal Tolls Act of 1845.

The government became worried that railways were close to achieving a monopoly on freight. Some canal companies were not allowed to carry goods, so the Canal Carriers Act in the same year changed the law. All canal companies were now permitted to carry goods, and could also lease other canal companies. The Leeds and Liverpool Canal company became carriers for the first time that year.

However, this law had an unintended side effect because some railway firms already owned canals, and were therefore 'canal companies'. Railway companies now had the power to buy or lease independent canal companies and their power base increased instead of declining. In north-west England, groups of railways joined forces and leased all the canal routes across the Pennines for several decades. This put the finishing touch to the textiles trade still carried by boat in this area.

By the mid-1860s, over a quarter of Britain's 4,000-odd miles of inland waterways were in the control of railway firms. For example, the Great Western Railway took over the Kennet and Avon Canal in 1852, and by the 1880s it also owned the Brecknock & Abergavenny Canal and the Monmouthshire Canal.

In a few instances, separate railway and canal companies co-operated to their mutual benefit. The Glasgow, Paisley and Johnstone Canal ditched its successful packet service in 1843 and let the Glasgow, Kilmarnock and Ayr Railway take over its passengers, on the understanding that the railway did not interfere with bulky freight traffic on the canal.

The government belatedly realized what was happening and passed the Railway and Canal Traffic Act (1873) to stop railways taking over canals in this manner, but the damage was already done.

The railway firms' greater capital resources made it difficult for canal companies to compete with them. For example, the London and North Western Railway owned 16 miles of canal (from Stourbridge to Birmingham) on which they charged 2s 0½d per ton for carriage. The Birmingham and Warwick Canal Co. then carried the same goods on to Warwick (a distance of 40 miles) at just 10d per ton, because they had to keep their prices in line with the rail companies' charges over land.

In the 1870s the railways' iron grip on goods transport caused increasing disquiet. Industrialists complained about the high cost of rail freight. Calls were made to modernize Britain's canals by widening some canals to produce a more unified system and reduce the amount of costly trans-shipping.

Canal companies made a number of improvements including the Anderton Boat Lift in Cheshire, designed by engineer Edward Leader Williams. The lift linked the River Weaver and Trent & Mersey Canal, which were separated by a 50ft height difference. The lift opened to traffic in 1875. At Foxton, where a staircase of ten locks caused traffic problems, an inclined plane was opened in 1900 but sadly was not a commercial success.

Transport costs at home compared unfavourably with those on the Continent and in America, which enjoyed more modern waterways communications. Many felt that nationalization or funding by local authorities were possible ways of meeting the huge costs needed to modernize waterways so they could compete with railways. Railway

A boat emerges from the Anderton Boat Lift onto the Trent & Mersey Canal, 1920s. Cassell's Book of Knowledge (*Waverley Book Co., n.d., c.1924*).

companies controlled over one-third of the waterways network by the early 1880s.

Worries about high railway freight charges in north-west England helped launch one of the last great engineering canal projects of the century. The Manchester Ship Canal opened to traffic on 1 January 1894. Some 76 million tons of rock and earth were excavated to complete its 35½-mile length. 'Steam navvies' were used to speed up the work, but even then over 16,000 ordinary navvies (men and boys) were employed at peak times. The Ship Canal was a great success, and waterways supporters believed it showed what could be achieved with suitable investment.

Despite the railways' success, the waterways were still used for carrying cheap, bulky freight until after the Second World War. However, two world wars and nationalization in 1948 left the waterways in a parlous state: underfunded and increasingly derelict.

'A lot of people gave up their boats' when the waterways were nationalized, Lily Wakefield remembers. Lily and her husband Kenneth have fond memories of growing up on the canals. The Wakefields belong to the generation that was the 'last of the boat people'.

Lily was born on a Mersey Weaver boat, the *Mersey*, at Longport (Burslem) on the Trent & Mersey Canal in 1934. She comes from a long line of boating families: her father James Wain was related through his mother to the Theobald family. Lily's grandfather Joseph Wain also worked for the Mersey Weaver Company. Her maternal grandfather William Carter owned his own boat, *Live and Let Live*, which worked on the Llangollen Canal.

Lily was an only child: 'I had a brother but he was stillborn. My mother got kicked by the horse when I was about two years old.' However, Lily 'had a wonderful life because I was brought up with family on both sides'. Lily lived with her grandparents a great deal, and grew up with her cousins around her. 'We were more like brothers and sisters'.

Kenneth Wakefield was born in 1932 on an Anderton Co. boat, *Margaret*, at the bottom of Runcorn locks. His father John and uncle Bill were twins; they were born on a canal boat at Etruria. Kenneth had one brother and two sisters. Their parents had a house on land. He recalls: 'It was a good life, a healthy life, but the worst part of it was education'. As we shall see later, it was difficult for canal-boat children to get an education.

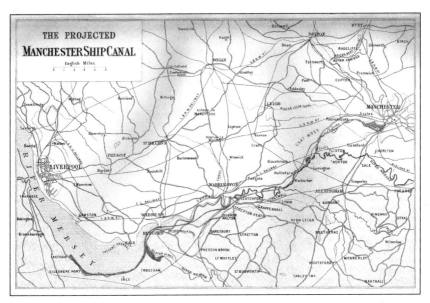

Projected route of Manchester Ship Canal. National Encyclopaedia, Vol. III (*William Mackenzie, c.1894*).

The killer blow to canal freight was the 'big freeze' of the winter of 1962–1963. Boats were locked in ice for weeks on end while lorries and trains kept on the move.

One by one the independent carriers closed down, and the national carrier, British Waterways, stopped carrying freight in 1987. The canal trade slowly ebbed away, and with it a traditional way of life for generations of families.

Chapter 2

KEEPING BRITAIN MOVING

An immense variety of vessels frequented Britain's inland waterways. By far the most common craft were the 'slow' narrow boats (monkey boats), which measured 70ft to 72ft in length and from 6ft 9in to 7ft 2in wide and carried cargoes up to 30 tons.

As noted earlier, boat dimensions were dictated by the size of the canals they navigated. On the Yorkshire canals there were 'short' boats, 58ft long and 7ft wide. These were specially constructed to navigate the locks on the Huddersfield Broad Canal, Calder and Hebble Navigation and Huddersfield Narrow Canal.

The Shropshire Union canal system was home to some specialized narrow boats only 6ft 2in wide. Yet another type of 'short' boat was found on the Leeds and Liverpool Canal because of the dimensions of the locks between Leeds and Wigan. These boats were 62ft long and up to 14ft 3in wide.

The Leeds and Liverpool had 'long' boats, 72ft long, which travelled between Liverpool and Wigan, and to Manchester and Runcorn after the locks at Leigh were altered to accommodate them in the early 1820s.

'Tub boats' carried coal on the Shrewsbury Canal and the Duke of Sutherland's Canal. Trains of these boats were towed by horse.

Day boats, like the coal boats on the Birmingham Canal Navigations, were used for short trips and did not have any sleeping accommodation. These boats were worked by men.

An early type of container system was used on some canals. On the Duke of Bridgewater's Canal, open-top iron boxes of coal were loaded by crane onto 'box boats', and this made loading much quicker and easier. The 'box-boat' system worked so well it was still in use in the first half of the twentieth century.

Sailing vessels were a common sight on the river navigations and some broad canals: there were Mersey and Weaver 'flats', Norfolk wherries, Yorkshire keels, Severn trows and Fen lighters, to name just a few.

There were massive Thames barges such as those on the Surrey Canal. These monster craft were 105ft long and 17ft 9in wide. 'Wide-beam' barges up to 11ft in width travelled on the Grand Junction Canal.

Bessie, *a cast-iron 'joey' boat at the Black Country Living Museum. Bessie was built c.1895 for the Harts Hill Iron Co. on the Pensnett Canal; her working life lasted right into the 1970s.*

Iron-hulled boats first appeared on the rivers Thames and Severn in 1810, but were more generally found on Scottish inland waterways (from the mid-1820s onwards).

In Scotland, the canals were mainly ship canals, apart from the Glasgow, Paisley and Johnstone Canal which was worked by a type of narrow boat 70ft long and 5ft 9in wide. Canal boats in Central Scotland were called scows and lighters. Boatmen on the Forth and Clyde Canal earned about 4s per day in the late 1850s. Boats on the Irish canals were called lighters, too.

Sending goods by canal was much faster than land carriage but inventors soon explored the possibilities of steam power. William Symington's successful trial of a steam boat on Dalswinton Loch in 1788 was followed by the launch of his *Charlotte Dundas* on the Forth and Clyde Canal in March 1802.

Unfortunately, the canal's owners were worried that the canal banks would be washed away by a steamboat's wake. It was not until 1856 that the first 'puffer', *Thomas*, appeared on the Forth and Clyde Canal.

The earliest attempt to power a canal boat by steam in England was probably an experiment in June 1793 by John Smith, a 'self-taught mechanic' from St Helens. The *Mechanics' Magazine* (1832) reported that the boat's first excursion, 'laden with passengers', was 'down the Sankey Canal to Newton Races'. Its next trip (to Runcorn and then along the Bridgewater Canal) had an unhappy ending. Thousands of people turned up to see this wonderful new invention and clamoured to climb aboard, so Smith began charging visitors to the boat to try to limit the numbers. An angry 'party of mechanics' got hold of the boat and 'almost destroyed her'.

In England steam vessels were more usually found on river navigations early in the nineteenth century but steam tugs were gradually introduced on some canals. The Birmingham and Liverpool Junction Canal Co. began towing 'trains' of boats by steam tug in 1844.

The 'Tom Pudding' or 'compartment' boats on the Aire & Calder Navigation from the early 1860s built on this idea. Instead of a box, the boat itself was the container and carried over 30 tons of coal. Long trains of Tom Puddings were pushed along by steam tugs. After the dawn of the twentieth century, tugs switched to towing the Tom Puddings instead. Motor boats first appeared on the inland waterways in the 1910s.

The fastest vessels on inland waterways were the 'fly' boats which carried very light, time-dependent items like fresh fruit, vegetables or fish. For example, Cheshire farmers' wives took their produce into Chester by boat. Fly boats had four-man crews (two on duty, two off) so they could work round the clock.

Passengers were a profitable sideline for canal companies. The Duke of Bridgewater began a packet service from Broadheath to Manchester in 1767, and extra destinations were added over the next few years.

In June 1801 the famous Paddington packet boats were introduced on the Grand Junction Canal after the Paddington branch was completed.

The passenger boats or 'track-boats' on the Forth and Clyde Canal were famed for their speed. Each boat was pulled by 3 horses and in 1818 more than 95,000 people used the service. The *New Statistical Account of Scotland* (1835) reported that in 1833, horse-drawn 'swift iron boats' were introduced on the canal which travelled at 'ten miles an hour'.

On the Royal Canal in Ireland, passenger boats between Dublin and Mullingar in the 1830s travelled at 7 miles per hour. Many passenger boats later fell victim to the railways, although the Gloucester & Berkeley

Passenger boats on the Paddington Canal, 1840. The canal first opened on 10 July 1801. Old and New London, *Vol. V (Cassell, Petter & Galpin, c.1890).*

Canal, later known as the Gloucester & Sharpness Canal, successfully ran steam services into the early 1930s.

Most boats were owned (sometimes hired) by canal companies and major carriers such as the Wigan Coal and Iron Co. on the Lancaster Canal. Men like the Duke of Bridgewater wanted to keep as much profit in their own pockets as possible after the huge investment they had made in their canals. The Bridgewater Trustees took over the running of the canal after the Duke's death but boats on his canal were known as 'Dukers' for decades afterwards.

Some canal companies tinkered with canal carrying for a while but gave up when profits eluded them. Others did not carry cargoes themselves and relied on tolls from the independent carriers who used their waterway as their main source of income. Carriers on a canal who did not work for the canal company were known as 'bye-traders' or 'bye-boats'.

Several canal companies set up a 'separate' carrying company controlled by their shareholders. The Grand Trunk's carrier was Hugh Henshall & Co. Thomas Pennant noted in his *Journey from Chester to London* that 'The proprietors of the Grand Trunk Canal have employed upon it about fifty boats, exclusive of those belonging to other persons … They are calculated to carry twenty-five tons each, and are drawn by one horse, for which the proprietors receive per mile three halfpence per ton'.

Hugh Henshall was James Brindley's brother-in-law and was also clerk of the works for the Grand Trunk (Trent & Mersey). Henshall 'successfully executed … the most difficult parts' of the canal's construction after Brindley's death.

Henshall & Co. carried for firms such as Wedgwood as well as the Trent & Mersey Canal Company. When the North Staffordshire Railway (NSR) took over the Trent & Mersey Canal in 1846, it set up its own carrying firm and Henshall & Co. was forced to close.

A large amount of capital was needed to build or buy a fleet and keep it running. In general it was rare for a boatman to buy his own boat and become a 'Number One'. The cost of a single narrow boat – over £60 in the 1770s – was well beyond the reach of an average boatman. A 'wide-beam' boat on the northern canals cost about £150 in the early 1790s. So a boatman was far more likely to hire his services to a canal company or independent carrier than be a boat owner.

However, there were significant numbers of owner-boatmen on canals in the Midlands in the closing decades of the nineteenth century, particularly in the Birmingham, Worcester, Oxford and Daventry areas.

It is difficult to say when horses were first used to help haul boats. Specially constructed towpaths for horses were only rarely found along early rivers. Later, teams of horses were sometimes required, depending on the tonnage of the cargo, or if the boat was navigating upstream on a fast-flowing river navigation.

If sails were not practicable, perhaps because of obstructions, boats were towed by teams of men called 'bow-hauliers' on some early canals and river navigations (some navigations such as the River Trent did not allow horse haulage until the 1780s).

In the canals' early days, boats were often left unmanned while the boatman drove the horse along. The boats would blunder into the canal banks or lock gates and damage canal property, so canal companies insisted each boat have a steerer as well as a boatman.

The animals used for motive power, 1870s. Drawing by Herbert Johnson for Our Canal Population (*London, 1879*).

In general, horses were preferred for narrow boats and some 'wide-beam' barges, and this practice continued well into the twentieth century. Pairs of donkeys ('hanimals' as the boaters called them) were used for haulage on the Stroudwater Canal, Worcester and Birmingham Canal and other waterways.

Fly boat companies like Pickford's kept teams of horses but a 'slow' or narrow boatman usually supplied his own horse. Some boatmen like Joseph Skinner, one of the last 'Number Ones' in the twentieth century and owner of narrow boat *Friendship*, preferred to use a mule.

Tracing Boats and Masters Before the Censuses

If you are looking for an ancestor who owned or was master of a large vessel on the inland waterways during the heyday of the canal area, his vessel may be on the shipping registers kept by Customs officers (CUST at The National Archives (TNA)) from 1701 onwards for ports in England, Scotland and Ireland. Local record offices may have the original registers for their area. From 1747, masters of ships had to keep crew lists or muster rolls (BT 98 at TNA).

In 1786 it was made compulsory for all merchant vessels over 15 tons to register with the customs house at their home port. Transcripts of these registers were sent to Custom House in London (Edinburgh for Scottish vessels). Unfortunately, the earliest copies or transcripts kept at London were destroyed in the early nineteenth century. The transcripts for the Port of London for 1818–1926 have survived (CUST 130).

TNA also has transcripts of the original registers of shipping and seamen from the customs records of London and Edinburgh (BT 107). Guides are available at TNA for these early shipping and seamen registers: Domestic Records Information Nos 92 and 94.

Another possible source for early boat names, owners and masters is Lloyd's Register of Shipping. This was a voluntary list of insured vessels; the records are kept at the National Maritime Museum. Some information from the register was published yearly. *Lloyd's List* (a weekly publication) gave updates of vessels arriving in port. The National Maritime Museum and Guildhall Library keep copies, and the Guildhall has an online database of shipping news from *Lloyd's List* from 1740–1837: www.cityof london.gov.uk/lloydsList.

In 1795 official registration began for smaller craft on inland navigations. An Act of Parliament was passed that required every boat over 13 tons on canals and other inland waterways to be registered with the clerk of the peace. A few registers have survived and are kept at local record offices. This legal requirement ceased following the end of the 1798 parliamentary session.

The ledger entry for each boat gives the name of boat owner (and sometimes the address), and the name of the boat's master or captain. The register also details the boat's normal route. Registers for Scotland do not appear to have survived. (There appears to be just one register for Wales, compiled by the clerk of the peace at Haverfordwest for the River Cleddau; it's held at Pembrokeshire Record Office.)

```
(Number  36  —  )

    IN Pursuance of an Act, passed in the thirty-fifth
Year of the Reign of King George the Third, intitled,
" An Act for requiring all Boats, Barges, and other
Vessels of certain Descriptions, used on navigable
Rivers, and on inland Navigations, in Great-Britain,
to be regiftered," John Gilbert of Worsley in the County of
Lancaster and Boundleus Bourne and Edward Mason off —
Liverpool in the County of Lancaster Merchants —
having this Day declared to me, Charles Bett (Deputy
Clerk of the Peace for the County of Chester, that —
Peter French   -   -      -     -     -    - -
is at present Master of the  Boat — or Vessel, called,
The  Marston   —— and that the said Boat ———
or Vessel, admeasures Thirty seven  -   -    -    -   —
Tons, and no more, and is at prefent worked by the Number
of Persons in the several Capacities under-mentioned,
videlicet,
```

Extract from the Register of Vessels, Chester, 1795–1812. Marston was registered at Chester on 24 August 1795. She was part-owned by canal engineer John Gilbert. All inland waterways vessels had to be registered with the Clerk of the Peace. CRO QDN/1.

The boat registers that have survived can be found in quarter sessions records for the relevant counties (see Section E). Although certificates of registration were issued to owners by the clerk of the peace, you are far more likely to find the registers.

Case Study 1

Vessel No. 22 in the Chester Register of Boats is the *Eliza*, a sailing 'flatt' (flat) owned by Thomas Barker of Northwich and registered by Charles Potts, the clerk of the peace, on 22 August 1795. *Eliza* was crewed by a 'Master and Hand' and the master's name is given as Samuel Bodson. The vessel was licensed to travel in the area of: 'Northwich ... to Liverpool in the County of Lancaster and up the Sankey Navigation' (CRO QDN4/1).

> **Case Study 2**
>
> John Gilbert (the Duke of Bridgewater's agent) had seven canal boats registered in his name at Chester. He part-owned the boat *Marston*, registered on 24 August 1795 as boat No. 36. The register gives a full list of *Marston*'s owners: 'John Gilbert of Worsley in the County of Lancaster and Cornelius Bourne and Edward Mason of Liverpool in the County of Lancaster, Merchants'. The master of the 37-ton vessel was Peter French; 'no other' crewmen were listed, and the boat usually travelled 'from Marston in the County of Chester to Runcorn' (CRO QDN4/1).

The 1795 Act expired at the end of August 1798, but several counties kept their registers going for a few more years. Extracts of the 1795 registers were sent to the Commissioners of the Admiralty, but these documents seemingly no longer exist. The Act was repealed in 1837. Women owned boats, too. Widow Catherine Horabin 'of Frodsham' had three 'flatts' registered in her name at Chester: *Mentor*, *Diligence* and *Liberty*.

Watermen (who ferried passengers) and lightermen (who were responsible for cargo) on the River Thames had to be members of a very ancient guild, the Company of Watermen and Lightermen. Canal carriers whose boats journeyed as far as the River Thames had to register their vessels at Waterman's Hall, and you may find old photographs of your ancestor's boat with a Waterman's Hall registration number.

Records for Waterman's Hall before 1908, including registers of barges and passenger boats, are kept at the London Metropolitan Archives. Only records after 1908 (when the Port of London Authority was formed) are archived at Waterman's Hall.

John Hargreaves was a well-known early canal carrier who moved goods by road and canal in the 1820s. It was Hargreaves' proud boast that he moved goods 'further than any man in England'.

Myles Pennington had fond memories of Hargreaves, who was a 'grand old English gentleman' resplendent in a 'massive gold snuff-box, heavy gold chain, with giant seals hanging from his fob, fine silk broad-brimmed hat' and an 'immense broadcloth black top coat' – a man of wealth and prestige in the community.

Hargreaves' fly boats sailed from Manchester and Liverpool to Walton Summit, where his goods were unloaded and sent across a tramway worked by horses to Preston, on the Lancaster Canal, where they were sent by canal boat to Lancaster and Kendal (and on as far as Scotland by waggon and cart). His boats 'could hardly be said to fly': they travelled at a stately 3 miles an hour.

John Hargreaves was a notable 'whip', and handled a coach and horses with ease. The firm's horses were a valuable asset, and if they became lame or poorly, they were sent to his Wigan farm where he 'doctored them himself'.

Other early carriers included the Thames and Severn Canal Co. and the Birmingham Coal Co., but Hargreaves' main competitor was Pickford's, which started out as a family firm.

James Pickford began carrying goods between London and Manchester by road in the 1750s. The company was quick to see the opportunities presented by canal transport and by the 1790s they owned several boats.

Pickford's sons Thomas and Matthew later inherited the business and the firm rented a wharf at Brentford. After the Grand Junction Canal opened the firm built warehouses at Paddington and began a regular service carrying cotton and other goods. The Baxendale family took over Pickford's after the end of the Napoleonic Wars, when there was a trade slump.

Their fly boats were crewed by a captain and three men. The firm had a high opinion of its workforce. Joseph Baxendale wrote they were all men 'in whom we can place trust and confidence, the property entrusted to their care being at all times very considerable'.

Pickford's carried human cargoes, too. It had a contract with the Board of Ordnance to convey soldiers and their families. The company provided plenty of clean straw to make the troops comfortable in the hold. Infants under 1 year old were carried free of charge, and older children under 14 were carried for half the price of an adult.

The Pickford papers at TNA contain a receipt from Thomas Paterson, an officer in the Royal Artillery, to 'certify that Thomas and Matthew Pickford & Co. provided boats for the conveyance of the company of artillery under my command and their wives children and baggage and that the same left Liverpool on the 8th February 1819 for London'.

Pickford's switched to rail and left the waterways in 1848 after becoming disenchanted with the comparatively high tolls on the canals. It later abandoned the railways for road haulage.

The famous canal carrying company of Fellows, Morton & Clayton (FMC) was another family firm, founded in 1837 by Joshua Fellows, a Staffordshire man. After his death in 1854 his widow kept the business going until her son Joshua (one of ten children) was old enough to become a partner in the business.

The firm was very successful. It had its own boatyard at Tipton and by the early 1860s the Fellows family had nearly fifty boats registered at Waterman's Hall in London and ran other trade concerns on the Thames.

Thomas Morton was an agent for the Bridgewater Trustees, and he also began working as an agent for Fellows in the early 1870s. Joshua Fellows (1843–1900) and Morton joined forces in 1876, and in 1889 the firm expanded further when a partnership was forged with William Clayton, a carrier at Saltley in Middlesex.

FMC carried many different types of cargo: turpentine, tea, sugar, cocoa beans (for Cadbury's at Bournville), iron, steel, etc. Its boats were called 'Joshers' by the boatmen in honour of Joshua Fellows.

Coal, the reason for the birth of the canal system, continued to be regular freight until the 1960s. Samuel Barlow's coal boats were a regular sight on the Grand Union Canal in the 1940s, although the company began switching to road transport after the Second World War. In the twentieth century, oil and petroleum cargoes were still important sources of income for the waterways.

Canal carrying companies had their own liveries: FMC boats were black and white until the early 1920s, when they switched to red, green and yellow paintwork with white markings. Thomas Clayton (Oldbury) Ltd, which carried oil and other cargoes in the Midlands and further afield during the twentieth century, had red, yellow and green boats with white markings.

Trade or street directories are useful sources for canal carriers; some date back to the 1760s. Pigot's 1822 *Commercial Directory for Cheshire* mentions goods were conveyed daily between Manchester and Ashton via the Ashton Canal, and a number of canal carriers are listed. The Trent & Mersey Canal Co. fly boats left Middlewich daily (the wharfinger was Jos. Smith). Goolden & Co. was one of the Nantwich canal carriers (agent James Tomkinson), and Coffield & Co. ran a daily service from Tower Wharf, Chester.

'Carriers by water' at the Canal Wharf, Stoke-on-Trent listed in William White's 1834 *History, Directory and Gazetteer of Staffordshire* include Pickford's, H. Henshall and John Kenworthy. The directory mentions the firms that clustered along the waterways and used them for transport. At Smethwick (west of Birmingham), the iron foundry belonging to Matthew Boulton's Soho factory and the Smethwick Brass Company were situated on the canal.

In addition to ordinary trade directories, maritime directories such as those by Thomas Marwood and others were published. John J. Mayo's *Mercantile Navy List and Maritime Directory for 1867* lists several canal companies. Their address, names of their vessels registered, registration number and tonnage, and port of registry are given. For example, the Grand Canal Co. (James Street, Dublin) has three steam vessels listed, the *Athlone* (36 tons), the *Dublin* and *Limerick* (each 34 tons), all registered at Dublin.

Early regional history and topographical accounts proudly tell the story of the growth of the local canal network and list the types of cargo carried. Publications such as these could help you trace the location of buildings if no traces of buildings or maps of a site have survived.

From William Pitt's *Topographical History of Staffordshire* (1817) we learn that at Uttoxeter: 'the wharf belonging to the Grand Trunk Canal company, with several large warehouses enclosed by a brick wall' was situated 'at the northern extremity of High St'.

Henry de Salis's *Bradshaw's Canals and Navigable Rivers of England and Wales* (1904) notes the location of canal wharves and company warehouses along each stretch of the canal network and names of the canal company's proprietors and important officers: managers, engineers, goods managers, secretaries, etc. De Salis lists each canal company under the name of the railway that owned it, where appropriate.

Canal Company Administrative Records

The canals and inland waterways network was mostly created by private enterprise, with just a small number of public works, as mentioned earlier. Records for public works such as the Royal Military Canal, built during the Napoleonic Wars, can be found at TNA.

Minute books recorded occurrences at canal company meetings. They cover a broad range of business activities from dealing with rival firms to insurance matters. Occasionally, minute books and correspondence may have information on individual boats or masters, especially if they had caused trouble for some reason such as theft or damage.

TNA has the largest collection of canal-company minute books. It has significant holdings of stock and share registers and other administrative records. The Gloucester Docks waterways archive has several canal-company minute books, engineers' minutes, staff lists and many other types of records. Local record offices also have company minute books, share records, staff records and other papers relating to the day-to-day running of each company.

Stocks and shares registers can be rich in biographical detail. If a shareowner married, died or passed on their shares to another person the change of ownership will be noted in the registers. There may even be copies of death or burial certificates or probate grants in the registers.

If you do not know where to start looking for a canal company, carrier or other canal-related business, you can use the National Register of Archives index, Access to Archives website and Virtual Waterways Archive as finding aids.

The National Register of Archives (NRA)

The register at TNA has over 40,000 catalogues and lists, some unpublished, of the location and types of material held in archives in Britain and abroad. The register is maintained by TNA: Historical Manuscripts Commission (TNA: HMC). Each business, person or estate on the register has a unique NRA catalogue number.

The NRA catalogues and lists can be consulted in the Open Reading Room in the library section.

The vast majority of NRA catalogues and lists are not available online but they have been indexed and can be searched at the NRA website: www.nationalarchives.gov.uk/nra/default.asp.

Prominent families and their members in the register include the Canal Duke, Francis Egerton, 3rd Duke of Bridgewater. A few NRA catalogues are available online and there are electronic links to them from the NRA website.

There are several ways to explore the NRA index, so do not be put off if at first you cannot find the business, corporate body or person you are looking for straightaway.

First, you can conduct a 'Simple Search' of the online NRA index by corporate name (companies and businesses), personal name (which combines the personal index, diaries and papers catalogues), family name and place name. (NB omit the 'Co.' part of a company name if you draw a blank at first when you search for a particular firm.) The 'Simple

---

Case Study 1 – Rochdale Canal Co.

The NRA index lists five repositories with records for this company. Greater Manchester Record Office has a large collection (B/2) dating from 1791–1968 which includes minute books, shareholders' records, ledgers, journals, cash books, receipt books, etc. Calderdale (West Yorkshire Archives Service), TNA, Birmingham Archives and Heritage Service, and Rochdale Archives and Local Studies also have holdings.

Search' does not search all five indexes at once, but there is an option at the bottom of the 'Simple Search' web page for each index to do more detailed searches.

For example, a 'Simple Search' of the NRA index by corporate name gives four locations (with links to their online catalogues) and the series reference numbers (where known) for Barnsley Canal Co. papers: TNA (RAIL 806), Sheffield Archives (115/B1-8), West Yorkshire Archive Service (C299) and Wakefield Libraries and Information Services.

If after several searches you still cannot find the company you are looking for, you can 'browse' the business index and organizations index alphabetically.

Case Study 2 – The Grand Junction Canal Company (GJCC)

An NRA index search of the corporate name index using 'Grand Junction' shows that TNA has a large collection for the GJCC under RAIL 830. More minutes and other records are in PRO 30/26. The London Metropolitan Archive has maps and deeds (701). Chiswick Library and Local Studies has the health register and other papers related to sanitary inspection. Warwickshire County Record Office has letter books and plans. Bedfordshire and Luton Archives Service has correspondence from the early 1800s in the Whitbread papers (W). The Science Museum Library and Archives has maintenance drawings (TECH D 303) and the Institution of Civil Engineers has some committee reports.

There is no guarantee you will find records for a particular company because papers may have been destroyed if the company went bust, the waterway closed or were just deemed too out of date to be of any use.

Each year TNA: HMC surveys new additions to Britain's archives and the new accessions published online. The accessions can be viewed by year, subject (e.g. transport) or repository: www.nationalarchives.gov.uk/accessions.

A2A: www.nationalarchives.gov.uk/a2a/

The Access to Archives (A2A) online portal can help pinpoint the location of thousands of different canal-related documents in local archives, record offices, libraries and educational institutions in England and Wales. However, please note the catalogue only contains information relating to roughly one-third of these collections.

Although A2A is extremely useful, the sheer wealth of information it generates can be daunting. For example, a search for 'Rochdale Canal Co.' elicits over 2,760 'hits'. Include as much information as you can in the search terms to help limit the number of results.

Restricting your online search to a particular time period using the 'advanced search' facility may be helpful. If you get a lot of 'hits', use the 'summary' boxes (by subject or by archive) to reduce the number of results.

You can also use the 'advanced search' facility on the A2A catalogue to explore one archive's collections at a time. This is particularly helpful for archives that do not yet have online catalogues, and those that do have online catalogues but are incomplete. Unfortunately, you cannot assume that all the holdings for a particular archive are listed on A2A. You may only be able to find the information you need by searching an archive's catalogues in person.

It is recommended that the reader uses both an NRA search and an A2A search when looking for canal-company records just in case one of the databases has not been recently updated.

You can use the Virtual Waterways Archive Catalogue (www.virtual waterways.co.uk/Home.html) to explore the records for British Waterways and its predecessors, including early canal companies and canal carriers. The database catalogues the collections held by The Waterways Trust's archives at Gloucester Docks and Ellesmere Port, and several partner repositories.

The Archives Hub index (http://archiveshub.ac.uk) is another finding aid for canal-company papers at specialist institutions and academic libraries.

Canal companies often changed their name or ownership over the years, for instance when taken over by railways, so you may have to check several sets of records to find the information you want. The records and minute books of railway firms that bought out canal companies often include useful information on waterways staff.

Canal companies did not merge very frequently, but there are some exceptions. The Ellesmere Canal Co. and Chester Canal Co. joined forces in 1813. In 1846, the Ellesmere and Chester, Birmingham and Liverpool Junction, Shrewsbury, and Montgomery Canals amalgamated to form the Shropshire Union Railway and Canal Company.

When looking for canal carrier records, use the same research techniques as for canal companies. However, records do not appear to be plentiful for small carriers. Use the NRA index, A2A and the Virtual Waterways Archive. A search on the NRA online index reveals that Fellows, Morton & Clayton papers are kept at Birmingham Archives (MS 454) but does not mention that the Gloucester Docks waterways archive has an FMC collection (BW118), which is listed on the Virtual Waterways website.

Solicitors' offices may hold a particular canal or carrying company's legal records. If you are trying to trace a current solicitor's firm which has evolved from the original firm that dealt with the company in question, the Law Society (www.lawsociety.org.uk) offers a research service for a fee (a substantial one).

None of these companies would have made a penny of profit without the boatmen who carried their cargoes. It is time to tell their colourful story.

Chapter 3

LIFE ON THE CUT

Who were the first canal boatmen? Where did they come from? At one time writers such as Tom Rolt theorized the boatmen were originally of gypsy (Romany) extraction. However, canal historian Harry Hanson made an exhaustive study of boatmen's names using the 1795 registers of vessels in *The Canal Boatmen* (1975). He found only a small percentage of boatmen with names suggestive of Romany descent, and concluded that 'very few' gypsies ever took to the boats.

St George's Chapel, Camberwell. An early view of the Surrey Canal. Note the lack of cabin accommodation. Gentleman's Magazine, *Vol. XCVII, January 1827.*

Historian Charles Hadfield speculated that the first boatmen came from a variety of backgrounds. They were perhaps agricultural labourers, or navvies who had worked on canal construction, or men already in the carrying trade, such as local farmers who earned money as a sideline by carting.

Journey times for boats were reasonably short at first, so little in the way of cabin accommodation was provided for boatmen, except in a few instances. Cabins became more common as more and more canals were cut, and boatmen became likelier to travel further. As the cargoes grew in value, a cabin was necessary so the boatman could stay on board all night and keep an eye on it.

Hiring arrangements were not uniform across the inland waterways system. On the largest boats, master and crew were paid by the boat owner, but on narrow boats, only the master (and sometimes the steerer) worked directly for the carrying company. The rest of the crew worked for the master, who had to supply his own horse and towing ropes.

The boatmen did not receive a regular wage; they were paid by the journey or the amount of cargo carried. This meant they were always in a hurry. Fly boats had priority on the waterways, and the quickest way to upset a boatman was to get in his way. Sometimes boatmen would race their boats to be first at a lock, and it was not unknown for them to come to blows with other boatmen or lock keepers.

The fly boatmen worked for very long hours. Eighteen-hour shifts were not unknown and the men rarely got a proper rest. These men could be away from home for several days at a time. A fly boat captain from Wolverhampton, say, might only get home on Sunday once every three weeks. Captain Randle, master of the fly boat *Stourport*, had a home in Stoke but only visited it three times a year.

Fly boat captains earned about £8 to £9 a trip in the early 1840s, but they had to find their men's wages out of this sum. The carrier Matthew Heath & Sons paid their captains £9 for a week's journey from Stourport to Manchester. The captains paid their crew members 7s per week, plus their meals. In the 1870s a typical wage for a fly boat captain per week was £4 17s 6d, from which he paid his men £1 a week each.

The slow boatmen worked for fourteen or fifteen hours each day before tying up their boat at night. They earned up to 30s per trip in 1841. By the mid-1870s wages had not changed significantly; in the Birmingham area, a slow boatman's wages averaged about 20s to 25s per week net after the expense of feeding and stabling his horse.

The boatman's horse worked the same hours, and was fed as the boat went along: 'They eat out of their nose-baskets while they are going through the locks; the horse stands a great deal of time [*sic*] while the lock is emptying or filling, and he just has to draw his boat a short way to the next lock, and during the time it is going through it has time to feed' (Select Committee on Sunday Trading, 1841).

Writer John Hollingshead travelled along the Grand Junction Canal on *Stourport* in the late 1850s. He wrote a series of reports on his journey for Charles Dickens's magazine *Household Words* in 1858 (later reprinted in *Odd Journeys In and Out of London*, 1860).

The *Stourport*'s crew of four (including its master Captain Randle) lived, slept and cooked in 'the smallest conceivable cabin' which was 'the model of tidiness'. 'One half of it is divided off for the bed, which rests under a wooden arch at the end of the cabin, immediately opposite the doorway'. Two men slept in the bed while the others worked. 'The bed rests in a perfect nest of cupboards, large and small, the doors of which are fitted with hooks that hold caps, brushes, and various small and necessary articles. The bed and clothes are very clean'.

A seat on one side of the cabin had storage space underneath. There was a stove by the cabin door for heat, and an oil lamp for light.

Hollingshead said the boatmen wore: 'short fustian trousers, heavy boots, red plush jackets, waistcoats with pearl buttons and fustian sleeves, and gay silk handkerchiefs slung loosely round their necks'.

There were few shops along the canals where boatmen could stock up on food. Captain Randle bought 50lb of beef before the *Stourport* set off. The meat was boiled straightaway to help it keep longer.

Boatmen did not spend all their time on the move. They routinely faced long delays waiting for orders, queueing at locks, and so on. Boatmen might be stuck hanging around at a wharf for days while their boat was unloaded and then loaded with a fresh cargo.

A Royal Commission reported that in Birmingham in 1876: 'the hay and straw boats, after a journey from Worcester and Gloucester of three days' often had to 'wait ten days until their cargoes are sold out: timber, salt and lime boats having to wait their turn to unload. They then go to Tipton, Hednesford, and other places to take in a return load of coal, and often have delay in loading; sometimes in frost for three weeks or more'.

If they were between trips, boatmen sometimes worked as porters at the canal wharves or as 'leggers' to earn extra money.

Tunnels like those at Blisworth or Harecastle caused major hold-ups. The expense of cutting canal tunnels was so great, as noted earlier, that some early tunnels like the Harecastle one were constructed without a towpath. Boats had to be laboriously 'legged' through the tunnels by the boatmen or by professional 'leggers' like 'Ben', who worked at Braunston tunnel for over five decades of the nineteenth century. Leggers' huts can sometimes still be seen near tunnel entrances.

The boatman's horse was taken over the tunnel while the men 'powered' the boat with their feet. The men lay on their backs head-to-head, so that each man's feet were on opposing sides of the tunnel. Then they pushed the boat along by 'walking' along the wall, one foot over the other.

It was miserable work. It took at least two hours to 'leg' a boat through the Standedge tunnel on the Huddersfield Narrow Canal, which was the longest in England. The boatmen sang hymns and songs to cheer themselves up. They had to stay awake in case they slipped off the boat and drowned in the darkness of the tunnel.

Sir George Head went by canal boat through Standedge in the 1830s: 'It is a hard service, performed in total darkness, and not altogether devoid of danger, as the roof is composed of loose material, in some parts, continually breaking'.

Winter was a bad time of year for the boatmen, especially if it was a harsh season: 'days and nights of exposure to drifting sleet, keen winds, and heavy snow, or cold, soaking rain'. If the canal (sometimes even the locks) were frozen, crews could be stranded for several weeks without the means of earning a wage.

Hollingshead reported that on the Grand Junction Canal in wintertime, 'alarming deputations of distressed bargemen' queued outside the house of one of the canal company's major shareholders, hoping for some charity.

Unusually dry weather could cause problems, too. On 7 November 1826 *The Times* reported part of the Leeds and Liverpool Canal 'between Kilnwick near Skipton and the vicinity of Burnley in Lancashire has not been navigable for several months' owing to a prolonged drought.

In his book *Canal People* (1978), Hanson called boatmen 'a rum lot', and it is only fair to say they acquired a mixed reputation during the nineteenth century.

Boatmen were not always squeaky clean when it came to other people's property. Early in the nineteenth century, John Hassell commented on the 'depredations (poaching) of the boatmen' on the Grand Junction Canal.

The canal ran through the Earl of Essex's estate, and the Earl employed a watchman whose job it was to see the boatmen did not steal anything as they travelled through his park. The watchman had a cottage ½ mile from Grove Mill bridge on the canal. A 'vista' or gap was cut through the trees that bordered the canal so he had a clear view of the boatmen as they passed through.

Unsecured cargoes were a great temptation to other boatmen along the canal (and the boatman conveying them). The *Legal Observer* (1839) reported: 'a more lawless class of men do not exist than the canal boatmen'. Cargoes were pilfered and the crafty boatmen used lots of different tricks to cover their tracks.

The police commissioner at Liverpool, Mr Dowling, said 'boxes and cases are broken open and plundered, and it is so well done that the discovery is almost a matter of impossibility until they arrive at their destination'. If goods went straight to the docks for export, it could be months before anyone realized there was something amiss.

The boatmen added water to cargoes such as coal so it was difficult to weigh accurately. They used special tools to tap liquid from barrels and then re-seal them so they looked as good as new. 'J. B.', a boatman convicted of theft, said: 'When boating I always took a little something of everything every journey'. The boatmen sold their ill-gotten gains to 'receivers' who lived along the canal banks.

Canal boatmen's reputation suffered greatly after the notorious murder of Christina Collins, a passenger on a Pickford's fly boat in May 1839. Three boatmen were found guilty of raping and murdering Christina. Two of them were hanged and one transported for life. Christina's death caused a great deal of debate on how to improve canal boatmen's moral condition.

Boatmen had no regular day of rest. Sunday was just an ordinary working day. They had an enforced rest while waiting for their next cargo, or if the canal froze up. They had no holidays, although when the canals closed at Whitsun for maintenance work they had their annual 'clearing out' of their boat.

Boatmen were accused of poaching, stealing, fighting and drinking. Many reformers felt this was owing to their lack of religious and moral education; they had no time to go to church or Sunday school.

The 1841 House of Lords Select Committee into Carrying on the Canals and Railways on Sundays (hereafter referred to as the Select Committee on Sunday Trading) was set up to see how widespread Sunday work was, and its effect on workers' morals.

John Crowley was a partner in the Wolverhampton-based carrying firm Crowley, Hicklin, Batty & Co. He gave evidence on the boatmen's character: 'Many of the boatmen are very trustworthy, honest, moral and sober' but added 'many of them are very much the reverse'.

Earlier in the century, there had been some missions to canal boatmen and watermen, reported in the *Christian Observer* (August 1818). In 1815, a clergyman who lived near one of the major intersections on the Grand Junction Canal began supplying boatmen with Bibles at reduced prices. The boatmen bought 'twenty-three Bibles and twenty-two Testaments' and expressed 'great satisfaction' with the new scheme. A small 'depository of books' was set up 'near the spot where the Aylesbury and Wendover branches fall into the Grand Junction Canal' (probably Marsworth locks).

The plan was so successful it was decided to extend it to the whole canal, where 'four or five hundred boats' were at work. On 20 March 1816 the Grand Junction and General Canal Association was formed; its patrons were the bishops of Durham, Norwich and Gloucester. Another 'depository' of Bibles was set up at 'Mr Harrison's Wharf on the Paddington bason [sic], and thirty of the Wharfingers were weekly subscribers to the Association'. Copies of the Book of Common Prayer were also provided to the boatmen either free or cheaply by another, anonymous donor.

London was home to several boatmen's missions over the years. In the late 1820s, the Paddington Society for Promoting Christian Knowledge Amongst Boatmen and Others opened a chapel at Junction Mews, Sale Street.

Four years later, a chapel was founded in Paddington for the boatmen on some Grand Junction Canal Co. land, which was initially leased and later bought from the company. Historian William Robins recorded that the Boatman's Chapel was constructed from an old stable and coach house 'by a few pious individuals who saw how much the poor boatmen' needed 'religious instruction'. The Chapel was later run by the London City Mission.

Following the Collins murder, there was a flurry of missionary activity on the inland waterways. In the 1840s, Lord Francis Egerton set up a flat (boat) as a floating chapel at Preston Brook which the boatmen could use on Sunday evenings, and was busy setting up another at Runcorn. At Chester, the Shropshire Union Canal Co. helped fund a boat with a spire to serve as a church for the boatmen and a school for the boat children. The firm of Henry Ward & Co. funded a floating chapel at Oxford, and the Old Quay Company founded one at Manchester.

The Staffordshire and Worcestershire Canal Committee helped fund a Boatmen's Friend Society in 1841 and this may be the Seamen and Boatmen's Friend Society reported by the FWAC in 1876. The society had canal-side missions at Manchester, Liverpool, London, Glasgow and Bristol and a 'large efficient school' at Severn Street near Worcester Wharf in Birmingham.

Many boatmen were in favour of stopping Sunday working but competition for work held them back. A boatman at Worcester Wharf said he would be 'glad to tie-up a Sunday, and rest like other folk' but he was afraid of losing work. If he didn't take the cargo 'others will' and he could not 'afford to lose a trip' (*Our Canal Population*, 1879).

Missionaries felt the canal network should close down on Sundays so the men could go to church, but canal companies did not really have the legal powers to shut their waterways to traffic.

The Select Committee's report did not lead to any specific legislation to stop Sunday work. It was left to individual canal companies and carriers to decide what suited their business (and conscience) best.

Carriers such as Whitehouse and Son at Dudley would not let their boats work on Sunday. The Calder and Hebble Navigation Company closed down one of its routes on Sundays and in 1874 the Shropshire Union Canal Company stopped Sunday work except for their fly boats.

The missions also set up refreshment rooms to try to wean the men from the pub for their social life.

Boatmen had the reputation of being heavy drinkers; they often stabled their horses overnight at the canal inns. The pub was their chief place of recreation. It must have been a relief to exchange the confined space of the cabin for a couple of hours in a warm, welcoming taproom. Mixed drinking was not encouraged; boatmen and boatwomen did not sit together. The boatmen loved to sing and dance while they enjoyed their ale: 'the big burly men are wonderfully light of foot, and keep time accurately' (*Our Canal Population*, 1879).

The ecclesiastical census of 30 March 1851 in England and Wales (HO 129 at TNA) surveyed churches and the number of people attending services in Britain. The returns may have information on chapels used by boatmen and their families.

The London City Mission Archive is held by the School of Oriental and African Studies (University of London). The British Library has some pamphlets and magazines on canal boatmen's missions such as the *Canal Boatmen's Magazine*. Birmingham Central Library has copies of the *Waterman*, another missionary leaflet. The Gloucester Docks waterways archive has some records for the Boatmen's Institutes at Brentford and Paddington for the 1920s.

Wendy Freer and Gill Foster's *Canal Boatmen's Missions* (Railway and Canal Historical Society, 2004) has a gazetteer of canal-boat missions, chapels and other institutions, and a detailed list of sources.

Critics of the Industrial Revolution commented on the break-up of the family unit as workers in industries such as cotton or wool moved from a domestic setting into the new factories. Life on the canals bucked this trend; families could live and work together. Although the majority of boats were worked by men and boys, a significant proportion were crewed by families.

A signal post on the canal. Drawing by Herbert Johnson for Our Canal Population *(London, 1879).*

There have been conflicting theories among canal historians about when and why families began living on the boats. Writers such as L.T.C. Rolt wondered if family boats originated when the canals were first built. However, Hanson used the 1795 registers of boat and barges (see Chapter 2) to show that only a tiny percentage of boat captains lived full-time on their boats. (It is not clear if their families were with them.)

Some writers suggested canal families first took to the boats for living accommodation when railway competition began to bite. But family boats were seemingly a common sight on the waterways many years before railways made a significant impact on the canal carrying trade.

The 1816 Paddington mission in the *Christian Observer* report mentioned earlier commented on the boatmen's wives and children. It estimated there were 'twenty thousand' men, women and children associated with the canal (including lock houses and 'engine houses'). These families 'may be said almost to live up on the water'. The mission discovered 'many of the boys who navigate them [the boats] and the children of the families who live in them [my emphasis], could not read'.

Hanson suggested boat families became more prevalent following the end of the Napoleonic Wars, when there was a trade depression. Jobs were in short supply as soldiers and sailors came home from the war, food prices were high and there was a shortage of housing. People faced a struggle to survive.

Canny boatmen realized if their families lived on board, they wouldn't have to pay any house rent. And if a boatman's wife or one of the children steered the boat, even more money could be saved because he would not have to pay a steerer's wages.

Four years after the defeat of Napoleon at Waterloo, John Hassell watched boats getting ready to journey through Blisworth tunnel on the Grand Junction Canal:

> Several barges were now preparing to enter the excavation; the men throwing off their upper garments and lighting up their lanthorn [*sic*], gave the helm for steerage to the women, one or two females generally attending each boat; when ready they loose the tow-rope of the horses, and apply themselves to the poles, with which they sturdily shove the boats through the dark channel.

These 'females' were almost certainly the boatmen's wives and daughters.

Witness evidence from the 1841 Select Committee on Sunday Trading showed that women had good reasons for travelling on the boats. They wanted to keep an eye on their husbands, as the Revd J. Davies commented: 'the Wife goes up with her husband as a sort of Protectress, to keep him from spending his wages'.

They probably wanted to stop their husbands from getting up to other kinds of mischief, too. Sir George Chetwynd, a retired chairman of the Trent & Mersey Canal, told the committee it was not uncommon for boatmen 'to hire females to accompany them on voyages, say from London to Manchester and back again'.

Life on the canals, although it was hard work, was seemingly more attractive than living in the dirty, congested towns because once families took to the boats, they stayed there.

The sons and daughters of the boatmen and women followed them on the canals. Boat boys became masters when they grew up, and boat girls married boaters. On the Lancaster Canal, several generations of the Ashcroft family worked on the boats.

It is difficult to locate accurate figures for canal boatmen and boatwomen or for the number of families living full-time on their boats until very late in the nineteenth century. Census data for the middle decades for inland navigation vessels was not gathered consistently, and can be unreliable. Women and children on board were not always recorded in the occupational data, even though they helped with the boat's everyday work. Day craft (where the boatmen kept a house on land) weren't included in the totals for people sleeping on board boats.

At Birmingham in the 1870s, the lock keepers estimated the proportion of family boats in their area as anything from one-third to over half the total number of working boats. Numbers may have fluctuated throughout the year. Families were more likely to travel with the boatmen during the summer, when the weather was warmer, and stay in their home on land in the wintertime.

Probably on average one-third of boaters lived permanently on board with their families, although the percentage varied across the canal network. Family crewed boats were most common in the Midlands. In north-west England, boatmen's wives and children lived on the Mersey and Weaver flats (boats), although they were more often found on

'Number One' boats. Keelmen's wives helped steer the boat or even did bow-hauling if money was tight and they could not afford horse hire.

In South Wales, Scotland and Ireland, boats were worked by men. On the Lagan Navigation in Ireland, some families lived on lighters but did not help the lighterman with his work.

In October 1875 factory inspector Mr Woodgate was asked to investigate whether women and children worked on canal boats in Ireland. He went on board boats travelling between Dublin and Ballina. Some vessels belonged to the Royal Canal and others to the Grand Canal. They all had male crews. Woodgate only saw one child at work: a 10-year-old boy at Athlone who said he did not receive any wages except his food.

However, Woodgate spoke to an un-named Dublin boatman who may have been working with his wife's help (contrary to Grand Canal Co. policy) because he said he 'would greatly prefer keeping his wife at home' if only his wages were high enough.

Another factory inspector, Mr Cameron, told the FWAC the following year that there were seventeen women and fifty children living on lighters in the Strabane Canal in County Tyrone, but they were not employed as workers.

In England the boatmen's wives and children were essential to the boat's efficient working. They worked for as long and hard as the men. The boatman's wife did the cooking, steered the boat or took turns with the older children driving the horse or donkeys along the canal bank. The wife and children also helped to load and unload the boat, which was extremely hard work. They were not paid any wages by the canal company. (However, if a boatman needed a 'big lad' to drive the horse, he hired and paid him.)

Families had a tiny living space on narrow boats and cabin size did not change markedly for most of the nineteenth century. Conditions were better on the wide-beam boats and barges on northern canals such as the Leeds and Liverpool. These boats had two cabins: the mate slept in the fore-cabin, while the captain and his family slept aft.

Even then, space was at a premium for large families with several children. A factory inspector found a family with seven children (the eldest was a 16-year-old girl) living in a boat registered at Runcorn with a cabin fore and aft.

Boatwoman at the tiller. Drawing by Herbert Johnson for Our Canal Population (*London, 1879*).

The cramped cabin conditions made it very difficult to keep children from harm. If the boat lurched suddenly, they might be burnt by the hot stove or scalded by spilt boiling water. And with so many people trying to sleep in a small space, there was always the risk that babies might be accidentally smothered by their parents. *The Times* (10 April 1877) reported an inquest at Runcorn after a child was found dead in a boat cabin. It had been 'overlain' by its parents.

Children left as they grew up and took up more room, usually when they were about 10 years old or a little older. If work was available, boys stayed with their father, working a boat alongside the family boat. They might be 'lent' to another family to help work their boat, or hired themselves to another boatman, perhaps on a fly boat. In a few rare instances, census records have been found of boys and girls as young as 11 and 12 apparently working a boat unsupervised with the help of younger siblings.

Girls might have to fend for themselves when they grew older, like 'Sarah T.', a 15-year-old boat girl imprisoned in Preston House of Correction in August 1840. Her story appeared in the prison inspectors' reports for 1841.

Cabin interior, 1870s. Drawing by Herbert Johnson for Our Canal Population (*London, 1879*).

Sarah was the daughter of a boatman and worked on his boat. When her father died, she helped her mother manage their boat, but for some reason her mother gave up working the boat. Sarah's mother went to live with another daughter, who would not let her sister stay with them. Sarah needed to earn her own living, so she hired herself to another boatman to 'drive and steer the horse'. She stole a watch from a farmhouse and got caught. The teenager told the chaplain at the House of Correction that she was 'instigated to the felony by the boatman'. Sarah was sentenced to one month's solitary confinement.

Sanitation on the canals was extremely primitive. There were no toilets on board the boats; people just used a chamber pot, and tipped its contents over the side of the boat. Even as late as the twentieth century,

Cabin interior from the bed. Drawing by Herbert Johnson for Our Canal Population *(London, 1879).*

few canal companies bothered to provide canal-side WCs for their workers. People hopped behind the nearest hedge for convenience, or resorted to the towpath if there was no cover.

Every drop of the crew's drinking water was carried in one or two large cans. If the water ran out, they had little option but to drink from the canal. Canal water was also pressed into service for washing clothes, which was often done on the towpath where there was more room than on the boat deck.

If a boat was stuck for a while waiting to go through a lock, the women seized the opportunity to start washing their husbands' shirts or their children's linen on the canal bank.

The canal companies did not lavish money on clean water and washing facilities for the boat families. The Grand Junction Canal

Company provided a standpipe at Brentford but not until the late 1880s. By the early twentieth century a few more had been installed elsewhere on the canal network.

Boatmen and their families were exposed to all weathers, but eyewitnesses commented on the 'robust vigour' of the women and children on board. The FWAC reported that the boatmen on the canals in the Warwick and Worcester areas were 'bronzed, healthy looking, and very superior in physique to the Birmingham working population'.

However, boat people had a far higher mortality rate than other workers in the open air such as farm labourers. They suffered from heart and lung diseases, rheumatism and circulatory problems. Many were prone to alcoholism.

Accidents were the biggest killer on the canals. Drowning was a major cause of death for adults and children; very few of them could swim. In March 1836 20-year-old James Hullock drowned in the Regent's Canal while steering a boat.

It was all too easy for a child to slip into the water's silent depths if both parents were busy. A 4-year-old child fell overboard and drowned at Camp Hill, Birmingham in 1875. Careful parents tied their youngest children to the boat deck so they knew they were secure. But older children helping their parents were inevitably put at risk: two children drowned on the Worcester Canal when they slipped while operating the lock gates one winter in the mid-1870s.

Great care had to be taken when loading a boat's cargo. The Theobald family suffered a terrible accident in the 1890s, which was reported in the *Northwich Guardian* (13 September 1893).

Boatman Tom Theobald was master of the boats *Ted* and *Willie*, owned by Thomas Hassalls of Ducie Street, Manchester. The Theobald family lived in the same street. The day before the tragedy, Theobald collected salt from Higgins' works at Anderton. The following morning (9 September) Theobald and his assistant Thomas Ditchfield went to Brunner Mond's works to pick up a load of soda crystals. The two boats were tied together by the canal bank. Thomas's wife and their four children were in the *Willie*'s cabin. *Ted* was empty, and lay next to the bank.

No one seems quite sure what happened next (the rope that fastened the two boats together may have unfastened). When Theobald and Ditchfield try to 'trim' (even up) the cargo of the *Willie*, the boat capsized. Mrs Theobald rushed out and screamed: 'Oh dear, Tom, whatever are you doing? The boat is going over!'

Tom ran into the cabin and grabbed two of the children. His wife slipped and fell in the water during the rescue but managed to climb onto another boat. Tom tried to save his other children, but it was too late: 9-month-old baby Lily and 4-year-old Elizabeth had drowned.

Danger was also present because boats travelled through the industrial heartlands of Britain. In the late 1880s, an unnamed boat family tied up their boat for the night at Runcorn. The man, his wife and two children

On the Bridgewater Canal. A canal horse seemingly used as a Derby racer like this would not have lasted long. Engraving by G.P. Jacomb Hood for Lancashire Historical and Descriptive Notes *(Seeley & Co., 1892).*

were sleeping soundly in their beds when chlorine gas escaped from a nearby chemical plant and entered the cabin. The boatman woke up and managed to get his wife and children onto another boat, but both children lost consciousness and never recovered.

Child labour is frowned on nowadays, but it was commonplace in Victorian Britain: work was all part of growing up. Children were employed in textile factories, coal mines, brick yards and workshops.

The boatmen's children were essential members of the crew on narrow boats. They drove the horse or steered the boat from the age of 7 or 8. Observers felt it was 'very healthy work for children of a proper age', although they might get hurt if the horse kicked them. Children sometimes got caught by the towing rope and were jerked into the canal and drowned.

When a canal boat went through a tunnel with no towpath, children were given the job of taking the horse over the tunnel while their parents legged the boat through. In June 1893, Sarah Jane Walker (aged 13) was left in charge of the horse with her 10-year-old brother William while her father and mother legged their boat through Saltersford tunnel on their way to Preston Brook (Trent & Mersey Canal).

When they were part-way through the tunnel, William shouted down one of the ventilation shafts that Sarah was in the water. When their horse was startled by another lad and his horse, Sarah held on tight to the towing line. She was dragged into the canal and drowned before her parents could reach her.

Sunday work meant children were unlikely to get the chance to go to Sunday school. Factory inspector Captain May made a 'Sunday voyage' from Stoke-on-Trent to Wheelock in Cheshire in the mid-1870s. He found that boatmen and 'large numbers also of women and children' worked more or less full-time 'steering, driving horses, or opening locks … debarred alike from the spiritual and physical blessings of the Sabbath'.

The boatmen's missions provided some educational facilities. One of the earliest schools for canal-boat children may have been the 1816 mission on the Grand Junction Canal mentioned previously. The missionaries were worried because 'many of the elder boys' spent their Sunday afternoons 'loitering about the boats and canal yard', and their language was 'most profane and offensive'.

They set up classes that were 'free to all the children connected with the barges, and the men who work on the banks and wharves of the canal. It consists of about one hundred and thirty children, boys and girls, together with several ... young men, about sixteen and eighteen years of age'. The 'young persons' learnt how to read 'the Scriptures and repeat the catechism', and classes ended with divine service. The classes were held every weekday evening and Sunday morning.

The 1840s missions also held Sunday schools. The boatmen's chapel at Kidsgrove in Staffordshire (Trent & Mersey Canal) had a Sunday school attached. The Worcester Wharf mission at Birmingham served as a day school and Sunday school and was still going strong in the 1870s. But many boat children had little opportunity to go to school and grew up unable to read and write.

Chapter 4

SMITH'S CRUSADE

Boat people felt they were a race apart. They were often ostracized by the people in the towns and villages they passed through because of their unfortunate reputation.

Yet the boat people had their own etiquette. A boat family's vessel was their 'castle' and it was very important not to intrude on another family's privacy. For example, casually stepping on board someone's boat in order to cross over to the canal bank was extremely bad manners. If you wanted to speak to someone inside a cabin, it was considered polite to knock on the door first.

Boatmen also felt 'different' because they had a language of their own: mucky, decrepit vessels were called 'Rodney' boats. Canal boats did not 'sail', they 'swam'. Like the navvies, boaters used nicknames or 'bye-names' such as Redman or Banbury Bess.

They looked 'different' from other workers, too. Boatmen sported bright neckerchiefs and beautifully embroidered belts and braces. The men on the Leeds and Liverpool Canal boats wore 'ganseys' or guernsey jumpers knitted by their wives.

Boatwomen were warmly and practically dressed, with a full-length skirt, a blouse, a pinafore to keep them clean and a shawl. They wore bonnets profusely adorned with long, heavy frills, which helped keep the sun off their heads and necks. When Queen Victoria died, boatwomen adopted black bonnets as a mark of respect, and this seems to have become 'standard' wear for some time among older women. Men, women and children wore stout boots or clogs.

Throughout the nineteenth century, philanthropists and reformers successfully fought for better working conditions and shorter hours for child workers. Factory and Workshops Acts limited working hours and ensured children had time to go to school.

However, children living on canal boats escaped notice. They did not live permanently in the towns they passed through, so local government took no interest in them. Women and children on canal boats were not covered by factory legislation. In addition, they were not directly employed by the major canal companies, so it was no one else's business how they spent their time.

In the 1870s, however, the condition of boaters and their children was brought under the spotlight thanks to the determination of one man: the self-styled George Smith 'of Coalville'.

George Smith (1831–1895) was the son of a brick maker. He grew up close to the canal at Tunstall in Staffordshire. When he was about 7 years old, he was set to work in the brick yard, where he was shocked to see children kicked and beaten to make them work hard. They spent their days covered in mud and carrying heavy lumps of clay for hours on end.

When Smith was older he established his own brick-making business, where he proved it was possible to make a profit without exploiting small children. Smith published a tract to raise public awareness of conditions in the trade. His *Cry of the Children from the Brickyards of England* (1871) caused a stir, and soon afterwards brick yards were brought under factory and workshop legislation.

In October 1873 Smith, now a seasoned campaigner, turned his attention to canal-boat families. He made many impassioned pleas to newspapers and magazines on behalf of boaters and their children. He claimed their cabins were filthy, overcrowded and unhealthy.

In order to generate maximum publicity, Smith did not hesitate to make the canal population problem seem far bigger than it was. He claimed there were 80,000 to 100,000 boat people, of which 72,000 were children. Smith reckoned 13,000 boat couples (over 50 per cent) lived 'in an unmarried state' and there were 40,000 illegitimate boat children.

In his book *Our Canal Population* (1879) he accused them of immorality: 'not more than two per cent are members of a Christian church'. 'Ninety-five per cent cannot read and write, ninety per cent are drunkards, swearing, blasphemy and oaths are their common conversation.'

They were certainly renowned for their colourful language. A writer in the *Daily Telegraph* (quoted by Smith) noted that a boatman's wife: 'is quite as much captain of the vessel as her husband. She can steer. She can hold her own with the man on the towing path. She can swear, and she does … the most horribly foul language it is possible to conceive.'

Smith called narrow-boat cabins: 'the most filthy holes imaginable', although he admitted some boat cabins were in 'apple pie order'.

He alleged boatmen's children grew up ignorant, neglected and abused: 'hundreds' were not 'taught to read and write, and fear God'. They were 'knocked from "pillar to post" – thrashed, kicked, and beaten

OUR CANAL POPULATION:

A Cry from the Boat Cabins,

WITH REMEDY.

NEW EDITION, WITH SUPPLEMENT.

BY

GEORGE SMITH, F.S.A.,

COALVILLE, Leicester.

London:

HAUGHTON & CO., 10, PATERNOSTER ROW.

Title page of George Smith's Our Canal Population *(London, 1879). Smith campaigned for years for better living conditions for 'boaters'.*

with ropes, sticks, and heavy-ironed boots, until many of the girls and boys become as stupid as the asses they drive'.

Smith's relentless crusade persuaded the government to put the 'floating population' under closer scrutiny. The factory inspectors were responsible for enforcing the provisions of the Factory and Workshops Acts to ensure child workers had the opportunity to go to school. But canals did not come within the remit of the inspectorate.

Factory inspector Robert Baker said he was first asked to investigate the boat people by Hugh Seymour Tremenheere (a pioneering school inspector and Poor Law commissioner) in April 1869.

However, there does not appear to be any concerted action until 1875, when the government set up the Factory and Workshop Acts Commission (a Royal Commission) to investigate how well current factory and workshop legislation was working. The factory inspectorate was asked to include the canal population in their report even though they were not covered by legislation.

First, the inspectors tried to establish if the canal population 'problem' in Britain was as vast as Smith alleged. Captain May estimated (from the 1861 census) that in England 'the number of persons enumerated in barges on canals was 11,915, consisting of males, 8,494, and females 3,421'. Separate figures for the number of school-age children were not available.

The Factory and Workshop Acts Commission (FAWC) reported in 1876. The inspectors found plenty of evidence to support Smith's accusations of overcrowding, lack of sanitation and illiteracy.

Living space in narrow boats had changed very little since the 1850s, as Captain May reported. A narrow-boat cabin 'is about 8½ft long, 5ft high and 6¾ft wide at its widest part. Within this space are frequently crowded at night a man and his wife and six children. I have known a case in which it was made to contain nine children besides the parents.'

The inspector was astounded that 'so many human beings can be stowed in so small a place, which contains, moreover, the cooking and domestic utensils, clothes, and provisions, in fact all the worldly goods of the family'.

Factory inspector Mr Richmond declared that narrow boats were 'utterly unfit for the numbers that live and sleep in them; I have myself seen families of eight packed into these dens …'.

The inspectors were not much more impressed by the cabins in the larger boats which carried bricks and manure in the Paddington and Brentford areas. Mr Henderson measured a cabin and estimated the living space as 800cu ft: 'about the space deemed necessary to each prisoner confined in a prison cell'. Yet a family of eight or nine lived in these 'wretched little hole(s)'.

These families had real problems with their floating homes because the cargoes they carried such as nightsoil or town refuse were extremely nasty. Rats were a real problem. If the bulkhead between the hold and cabin was in bad repair and leaked, smells or vermin could contaminate the cabin and living conditions became 'altogether indescribable'.

To get rid of bugs, boats were fumigated or 'stoved' while the whole family camped out on the towpath. In later years boats were fumigated at the company depot.

Where did they all sleep? A boatwoman in the Midlands with six children showed George Smith how they managed in a narrow-boat cabin. There was a 'table in front of the fire (stove) … three children slept on that, two lay under the bed where the parents slept, and two in a little cupboard above'.

Conditions in each cabin differed according to family circumstances and their character. Many families kept their cabins spotless and used water from the cut to keep canal boats' paintwork dirt-free.

George Smith included a report from the *Birmingham Daily Mail* in his book. The unnamed reporter visited some canal boats at Worcester Wharf at Birmingham in early March 1875. The first boat he entered had a three-man crew. 'Every inch of space' was utilized, with 'small cupboards, pigeon-holes and shelves' everywhere. The cabin, heated by a 'fat little stove in full glow', was a 'crowded and very hot … slovenly den'.

But the next floating home the reporter entered belonged to an old couple who owned their own boat and traded from Birmingham to 'Worcester and the Black Country'. The boat cabin was adorned with 'brasswork and tinware … in the highest state of polish … Some gay scraps of fringe decorate the beams of the bed place, and mourning cards of deceased relatives are hung about'.

Next the reporter climbed aboard a boat that was home to a family with five children. The cabin was 'dingy', but the couple's 1-month-old baby was 'dressed in a nice, clean white frock … the babies always seem to command clean and even gorgeous apparel'.

Another 'family boat' further along was 'very smart and cheerful'. This family kept a small house at Worcester to which they could retreat if any of the children were ill. It was 'a great expense to us' the boatwoman told

When Death steps in how much we need each other's kindly aid ;
So help the mourning friends that's left to place him in the grave ;
It is for this I now appeal to those who round me stand,
Then forward come in trial's hour and lend a helping hand.

THE DUKE OF HILL,

South Wharf Road, Biddington.

A FRIENDLY MEETING

Will take place at the above house on Saturday, April 21,

For the benefit of T. DIXON,

To help Defray the Funeral Expenses of his Boy.

Chairman—R. Allingham.   Vice—Bandy Vaughn.
Clerk, Dick Sivers.

Assisted by D. Kempster, T. Joyce, T. Garner, T. White-
house, G. Wileman, J. Tomlin, W. Darvill, H. Morgan, E.
Rudge, J. Nixon, W. Nixon, T. Clarke, T. Noone, S. Rudge,
C. Bishop, J. Bishop, and many others.

To commence at 8 o'clock.

'Nearly a copy' of a mourning card sent to boatmen asking for help for a 'poor boater' who had lost two children to smallpox. ('Biddington' is probably a euphemism for 'Paddington' to protect the family's privacy.) Our Canal Population (London, 1879).

the reporter, 'but you never knows [sic] what will happen, and my man and me likes [sic] to keep it on'.

Some families paid for glass to be fitted to their cabin roof, which made the cabins brighter. The light streaming through the window at night made the boat easier to see if the family needed to get on and off the vessel.

The canal companies disputed Smith's statistics on canal families. There seems little doubt that in his eagerness to engage the general public in his crusade, he wildly exaggerated the number of boat people in Britain and, a few years later, he quietly downsized his figures.

It is unlikely there were more than 40,000 people at work on inland waterways even if river boatmen were included. Author Harry Hanson, using the 1881 census and other data, believed a maximum figure of 30,000 people working on canal boats in England, including women and

'It glides slowly on', a canal boat family in the 1880s. Cassell's Family Magazine, *1883.*

children, was a reasonable estimate. Hanson thought it unlikely that more than 9,000 (probably less) people lived full-time on their boats, around one-tenth of Smith's estimate.

George Smith also gave a false impression of boat people's 'immorality'. Most boat couples, contrary to his allegations, were married.

However, Smith's accusation that boaters were illiterate was well founded. Education was still a particular problem for boat children because they were never in one place long enough to attend school regularly.

If a boatman wanted his child to go to school, there might not even be a Sunday school within easy reach of the canal, never mind a day school. Factory inspector Mr Johnston told the FAWC in 1876 that at Hednesford (Staffordshire), which was 'a great coaling place', there was no 'school, church or chapel within several miles'.

Some boat people were keen to get their children into school. Captain Randle on the *Stourport* made sure his son 'larn [*sic*] to read an' write'. Randle used to work for Pickford's, and when they sold off their canal-boat fleet the firm offered him a job as a railway porter, but he turned it down. He believed if he had been literate, the company might have found him an office job.

The Shropshire Union Railway and Canal Co. (SURCC) took a straw poll of its boatmen in 1875 to see how literate they were. Only one of eleven boatmen, 26-year-old W. Griffin, was able to read and write a little, and he was the only worker not brought up on a canal boat.

Forster's Education Act of 1870 and subsequent legislation had established the principle that every child should go to school. But it was difficult for school boards to enforce the Act if children had no permanent address.

Education was not compulsory for 5 to 10-year-olds until Mundella's Act of 1880. Parents had to pay for children's schooling unless they could prove they could not afford it. Only Sunday schools and some charity schools gave free lessons. Education was not free for all children until the 1940s.

On average, education at a day school cost a penny a day in the mid-1870s. Some boatmen willingly paid some pennies for their children's education if their boat was tied up for a few days.

If boatmen had a house on land, their children were more likely to go to school from an early age, but once they reached the age of 8 or 9 they were set to work on the boats.

The parents of many canal children did not see any point in sending their children to school. Their future lay on the boats, and their parents believed they learned everything they needed to know by helping them.

Workers in other occupations were prosecuted under the Factory and Workshop Acts if they kept their children away from class, but legislation designed for factories was pretty useless when an itinerant population was involved. A rare exception was on 31 March 1874, when Ormskirk magistrates fined three Burscough boatmen 5s 6d each for neglecting to send their children to school. One of the boatmen, Fairhurst Baybutt, is listed in the 1871 census living in a canal boat with his wife Eliza and their two daughters.

Several factory inspectors suggested the only way to get canal children into school was to ban them from the boats altogether. But this would have separated children from their mother: anathema to Victorian ideals of home and family. An alternative idea was the draconian step of stopping women from sleeping on board boats (which would have had the knock-on effect of removing the children, too).

Canal companies were reportedly against banning family boats. Their profits were under threat from the railways, and it was more economical for the company if families worked the boats, because the company only paid one wage for each boat. The FAWC was told it would 'ruin the canal carrying trade' if families were forced off the canals.

Some factory inspectors felt school boards should have powers to insist on boat children being sent to school. But was this a practical suggestion? One writer quoted by Smith suggested a truancy officer bold enough 'to ask the bargees [sic] what they might consider impertinent questions … would speedily learn the depth of the canal from personal demonstration'.

As we shall see later, attempts to bring more canal-boat children into the education system had little effect. Smith had more success with his crusade to reduce overcrowding on narrow boats. His campaign, aided by the FAWC report and evidence from the factory inspectors, nudged a reluctant government into action.

A Canal Boats Bill was introduced into Parliament in May 1877 by Mr Sclater Booth, president of the Local Government Board. The Canal Association (a manufacturers' association) petitioned against the bill, and a Select Committee was appointed to investigate Smith's claims.

Smith was greatly upset, and afraid his mission was doomed. But after much arguing among politicians, his long campaign on behalf canal-boat families bore fruit at last.

The Canal Boats Act became law on 14 August 1877 and came into force on 1 January 1878. This new legislation, which only applied to England and Wales, regulated living conditions on canal boats used as 'dwellings'. It did not apply to vessels registered under the 1854 Merchant Shipping Act which were working on inland waterways.

Every canal-boat owner must now register his vessel with a specified local authority. The Local Government Board (LGB), which was responsible for overseeing sanitary regulations and other legislation on a regional basis, appointed Medical Officers and Inspectors of Nuisances.

A section of the Canal Boats Act, 1877. Our Canal Population (*London, 1879*).

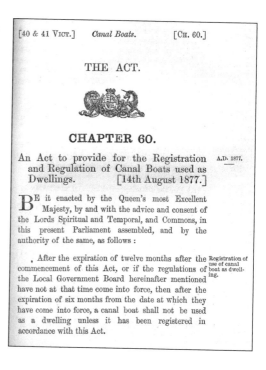

[40 & 41 Vict.]   *Canal Boats.*   [Ch. 60.]

THE ACT.

CHAPTER 60.

An Act to provide for the Registration and Regulation of Canal Boats used as Dwellings.   [14th August 1877.]   A.D. 1877.

BE it enacted by the Queen's most Excellent Majesty, by and with the advice and consent of the Lords Spiritual and Temporal, and Commons, in this present Parliament assembled, and by the authority of the same, as follows :

, After the expiration of twelve months after the commencement of this Act, or if the regulations of the Local Government Board hereinafter mentioned have not at that time come into force, then after the expiration of six months from the date at which they have come into force, a canal boat shall not be used as a dwelling unless it has been registered in accordance with this Act.   Registration of use of canal boat as dwelling.

It set up seventy-six canal-boat registration authorities. For example, craft on the Coventry Canal were registered with the Coventry Urban Sanitary Authority.

The LGB set minimum standards for accommodation in canal-boat cabins, and all new boats had to comply with the regulations. These stipulated 60cu ft of air space for each person over the age of 12, and not less than 40cu ft for children under 12 in every boat cabin. The sexes should be segregated where appropriate. Where 'foul or offensive cargo' was carried, the boat must have a strongly built double bulkhead to help protect the family from any leakage or vermin.

Sanitary inspectors were appointed by the local registration authority to inspect the boats. Now families would face regular inspections of their floating homes by officialdom: an unprecedented intrusion into domestic life.

Each boat's registration number and the name of the place where it was registered must be clearly displayed. In some areas the registration place name was represented by an abbreviation or a symbol so the inspector could see at a glance where the boat came from. Boats registered in

Liverpool sported a 'liver bird' and Chester boats often bore a wheatsheaf (from the city's coat of arms).

Sometimes a canal passed through more than one authority's jurisdiction. For example, Leeds and Liverpool Canal boats travelled through areas controlled by the Liverpool, Wigan, Blackburn, Burnley and Leeds sanitary authorities. However, a boat owner only needed to register his boat at one place.

Companies with fleets had boats registered at several places (each boat was only with one authority). Thomas Hales, traffic manager for the Shropshire Union Railway and Canal Co. (SURCC), gave evidence to an 1884 Select Committee on canal boats.

SURCC owned 400 narrow boats, the 'largest number of any carriers in the kingdom', 116 'flats and floats', 7 canal steamers and 3 river steamers (the latter did not come under the 1877 Act). The company registered its boats at Chester, Nantwich, Ellesmere and Welshpool.

These inspections could be very time-consuming. At Leeds, where 326 boats were registered during the 1880s, the medical officer of health needed an assistant, Mr Burton, who checked the boats weekly.

Procedures were put in place in case the inspector found any contagious disease on board. Smith (and some doctors) had accused canal boats of being sources of contagion, carrying disease into the hearts of towns. As boats came under regular scrutiny by the sanitary authorities, happily these worries proved largely unfounded, although there was a scare in Barnsley in 1883 when a case of smallpox was reported on a canal boat from Hull.

The new Act also tried to secure an education for boat children. The school board in the area where a family's boat was registered was made responsible for the children's education. Canal companies were given powers to build schools for the boaters' children if they wished.

George Smith was very unhappy with the 1877 Act because it was 'permissive' legislation. Sanitary authorities were given powers to ensure the Act was obeyed, but they were not compelled by government to implement the legislation. He was convinced the Act would be a failure unless the sanitary authorities and their inspectors were regularly checked by government officials.

Smith's suspicions were soon proved correct; the 1877 Act achieved very little in the way of improving overcrowding. He went on the warpath again, and demanded fresh legislation to address the Act's shortcomings. With the help of a sympathetic MP, Henry Broadhurst, a fresh Canal Boats bill was launched in the House of Commons. The bill proposed a ban on Sunday work for children, and yearly registration fees for boats.

The canal companies jibbed at the new bill; they felt annual registrations would be expensive. A House of Commons Select Committee on the Canal Boats Act investigated the canal network and living conditions and produced two lengthy reports, one in 1883 and another the following year.

The 1884 report found that several years after the Act's passage, some registration authorities had 'done very little' to implement it. They had not even started a canal-boat register, never mind appointed an inspector. Leeds was one of the more diligent local authorities.

Hugh Owen, the secretary of the LGB, gave evidence that 8,077 boats had been registered in England and Wales with accommodation for a total of 33,795 people, including children, since the 1877 Act was passed. (This figure does not give us the total number of boat people because a large number of these boats had been cut up since first registered. And day boats not being used as 'dwellings' did not have to be registered under the Act, so these boatmen were not included in the statistics.)

There were problems with the new law even in areas where health inspectors had been appointed. Not all canal boats used as homes had been registered because if a boat passed through several sanitary districts, it might escape notice. By 1884 there had only been 397 prosecutions under the 1877 Act.

It was easy for boatmen to hoodwink an inspector. If a boater had too many children on his boat, and he knew an inspection was imminent, he might pop a child on another boat until the inspector was out of sight, or send the child for a walk along the towpath until the 'danger' was past.

The Select Committee recommended that the 1877 Act needed beefing up, and it was accordingly amended, although not to the extent Smith wished.

The 1884 Canal Boat Act compelled local authorities to appoint sanitary inspectors to ensure boats complied with the new regulations, were clean and well maintained.

Merchant vessels used as 'dwellings' on the canals (such as Medway ketches, Thames barges and Norfolk wherries) now had to register as 'canal boats'. Fly boats could not be crewed by boys under 12 years of age.

When a boat was registered by its owner (who paid a fee), the owner was issued with two certificates, one of which was kept with the boat. These registration certificates tended to get rather dog-eared over time,

THE LOCAL GOVERNMENT BOARD.
CANAL BOATS ACT, 40 & 41 VICT.

Registered Mark N.D.
Registered No. 12160.

A BOATOWNER'S CERTIFICATE OF REGISTRATION.

The Sanitary Authority for of in the County of .

		Feet	Inches
Size of Cabin	Height	..	..
	Width	..	..
	Length	..	..
Other Living and Sleeping Accommodation	Height	..	..
	Width	..	..
	Length	..	..
TOTAL			

NUMBER ALLOWED TO LIVE AND SLEEP ON BOARD.

Women	....
Men	....
Females between the ages of 5 and 18	....
Males between the ages of 5 and 18	....
Children under 5 years old	....
TOTAL	

Name of Boatowner ....
Place of Abode ....
Date of Certificate ....
Signature of Sanitary Inspector .. ..

Canal Boats Act, 40 & 41 Vict., 1877.

Registered Mark N.D.
Registered No. 12160.

THE LOCAL GOVERNMENT BOARD, WHITEHALL, LONDON.

A BOATOWNER'S CERTIFICATE OF REGISTRATION.

WE, the Sanitary Authority for the of , in the County of , by the powers vested in us by the Canal Boats Act, 1877, do hereby grant a Certificate of Registration to Mr. , residing at , in the parish of , in the county of , for his boat named , Registered Mark , No. , to ply or let out for hire to or in any part of the country, for the year ending Whit-week, 18 . The living and sleeping accommodation being subject to and in accordance with the provisions of this Act, and the regulations of the Local Government Board for men, women, females between the ages of 5 and 18, males between the ages of 5 and 18, children under the age of 5.

Given under the common seal of the said Sanitary Authority, this day of , in the year of our Lord one thousand eight hundred and .

Signature of Sanitary Inspector

N.B.—In case this boat is sold or transferred, notice to be given at once to the Sanitary Inspector for the district which the boat is registered or belonging to, so that the purchaser's or owner's name and address may be entered upon the back of this Certificate.

All convictions to be entered upon the back of this Certificate.

Facsimile of a blank boat owner's registration certificate under the Canal Boats Act, 1877.
Our Canal Population (*London, 1879*).

but a few are still extant (the Gloucester Docks waterways archive and a few other repositories have some examples).

The health register records are in the form of large bound books, or card indexes or a bundle of boat certificates. They usually have an index with the names of boats and their numbers. If you know the name of your ancestor's boat, e.g., *Emerald*, you can check for its name in the index and then turn to the relevant page. (Some boat register indexes are more complicated than others, depending on the local authority's system.)

Occasionally boats are indexed by the company that owned them. For example, the Nantwich register has a simple numerical index, and also lists the Shropshire Union Railway and Canal Co. boats in an additional index.

The boat's entry in the register gave the date the boat was first registered, its owner's name and address, the master's name, the place where the boat was registered for the purposes of the Education Acts, its registration number, listed the type of boat (e.g. fly boat), specified the number of people it was permitted to carry and the cabin dimensions and capacity. The register also included the boat's usual route and the type of cargo carried.

Canal Boats Act,
40 & 41 Vict.

THE LOCAL GOVERNMENT BOARD, WHITEHALL, LONDON.

REQUISITION FOR A MASTER BOATMAN'S CERTIFICATE.

To be signed by the Applicant and a Respectable Householder.

I hereby request the   Sanitary Authority for   , to grant me a Certificate of Registration as Master or Captain of a boat named   , No.   , and belonging to   , residing at   , in the County of   , to ply for hire in any part of the country for the year ending Whit-week, 18   , in accordance with the provisions of the Canal Boats Act and the regulations of the Local Government Board. It is thoroughly clean, no infectious diseases on board, properly ventilated, and in a habitable condition. And I hereby further declare that I have not been convicted before any of Her Majesty's Justices of Peace for a violation of the Act.

     Dated this   *day of*   , 18 .

                     Name and Surname

                     Place of Abode

DECLARATION OF A RESPECTABLE HOUSEHOLDER.

I hereby declare that the applicant is a respectable man, and the above statements, to the best of my knowledge and belief, are correct.

     Dated this   *day of*   , 18 .

                     Name and Surname

                     Place of Abode

Facsimile of a requisition form for a master boatman's registration certificate under the Canal Boats Act, 1877. Our Canal Population (*London, 1879*).

Case Study 1 – **Alaska**

This horse-drawn fly boat was No. 807 on the Runcorn boat register. This narrow boat was owned by the Anderton Co., Stoke-on-Trent. It had one cabin and was licensed to carry four persons. *Alaska* was first registered on 4 June 1884, and its master was James Smallwood. It carried 'general' cargoes and its customary routes were 'the Bridgewater and adjacent canals'. Its cabin was 5ft high, 9ft 6in long and 6ft 5in wide, and it had 243ft 10in of 'net cubical capacity of free air space' (CRO LUR/57/5).

When a sanitary inspector (or official canal-boat inspector) checked a boat, its master produced the registration certificate so the inspector could make sure it was not overcrowded. Each sanitary inspector kept a notebook or pocket book in which he noted the date, boat inspected, the nature of its cargo, number of people on board, the children's ages (if present) and if they were boys and girls. He made a special note of any problems found with the living accommodation, or if any of the family were ill. The notebook entries were later checked against the boat registration ledger and written up into a large ledger or journal.

Case Study 2 – Runcorn Health (Canal Boat) Register – Edward

This boat, No. 835 registered at Runcorn on 13 February 1886, belonged to the Eureka Salt Manufacturing Co., Anderton, Northwich. Its master was Henry Smalley, and its cargo was coal and salt on the 'Bridgewater and adjacent canals'. *Edward* was a 'wide' boat with one cabin 3ft 9in high, 9ft 4in long and 5ft 3in wide with a net cubic capacity of air space of 183ft 9in (CRO LUR/57/5).

When the inspector found a boat that contravened the sanitary regulations, he contacted the boat's owner. Some authorities kept separate books for complaints or 'breaches' of the Canal Boats Acts. These books had detachable certificates with counterfoils. The inspector sent a complaint certificate to the owner, specifying the boat's name, master's name, date inspected and the nature of the problem found (e.g. leaky boat, overcrowding). When the problem was rectified by the boat owner, the certificate was recalled and fastened back in the complaints book next to its counterfoil along with a note of the date.

If an inspector's journal, notebook or the health register has survived (and assuming the inspector made accurate entries), we can build up a

---

Case Study 3 – Northwich Canal Inspector's Pocket Book

On 16 December 1947, the inspector visited the narrow boat *Dee* registered at Stoke-on-Trent, registration No. 932. *Dee* was owned by the Mersey Weaver carrying company at Port Vale Wharf, Burslem, and its captain was Charles Powell. It was licensed to carry three adults, and Powell's wife and two children lived in the aft cabin. (The children were both 10 years old, presumably twins, but their sex is not given.)

The cabin was 'clean' but the *Dee* was in a poor state of repair. The inspector commented it was 'not known' when the cabin was last painted. The cabin roof was leaking; the food cupboard had a broken door and was also letting in water. The inspector sent a letter of complaint to the owner on the same day he inspected the boat (CRO LUNo 3899/7).

---

picture of the family or crew on a boat, and its owners, during the time it was registered with a particular authority.

George Smith died at Crick on 21 June 1895. The last few years of his life were spent trying to ensure gypsy children were covered by the Education Acts, but he did not achieve the same success as with brick-yard and canal-boat children.

The Canal Boats Acts were his true legacies, and they did a great deal to improve living conditions for canal-boat families. The 1888–1889 report of the LGB noted: 'The indecent herding together of men, unmarried women, and children in barge cabins has been much diminished … The sanitary condition of the boats has also been substantially improved'.

The Canal Boats Acts of 1877 and 1884 were amended slightly in 1925, and superseded by the Public Health Act of 1936, but overall the sanitary regulations for canal boats remained virtually unchanged.

The 1884 legislation proved disappointing, however, with respect to education for canal-boat children. Concerns about boat people's illiteracy continued and their unique way of life was repeatedly called into question. The new century brought not only fresh challenges for boat people, but immense changes on the canal network. The waterways would never be the same again.

Entering a lock. Drawing by Herbert Johnson for Our Canal Population (*London, 1879*).

Chapter 5

'CUNNING MEN'

The first canal workers were the engineers and navvies who transformed Britain's landscape. When James Brindley was born, there was no recognized calling of 'civil engineer' as such. By the time of his death it was a highly respected profession.

The men who built Britain's canals came from a variety of different backgrounds. Brindley was the son of a farm tenant near Tunstead in Derbyshire. This self-taught genius started his career as an apprentice to a millwright at Macclesfield. After Brindley worked on the Bridgewater Canal and Trent & Mersey, he was in high demand for many other projects. He travelled day in, day out in all weathers, and wore himself out. One fateful day he got soaked while surveying a canal, caught a chill and died shortly afterwards.

John Smeaton was a scientist and instrument maker who won fame for his construction of the Eddystone lighthouse before he turned his hand to canals. He was involved in the Calder and Hebble Navigation, the Forth and Clyde Canal, Aire & Calder Navigation and others. It was Smeaton who first founded a society for civil engineers in 1771.

John Rennie (1761–1821) was a wealthy farmer's son who went to university; his first job was as a millwright. The Kennet and Avon Canal, Lancaster Canal and Crinan Canal were just a few of the many schemes he worked on.

Thomas Telford (1757–1834) started out as a journeyman mason and worked on Somerset House in London before moving on to an illustrious career as canal and road builder.

Engineers like Brindley and Rennie made a fortune from their work, but others such as John Longbottom, who worked on the Leeds and Liverpool Canal and designed the spectacular 'Bingley Five Rise' series of locks, died in penury.

Right from the planning stages of a canal project, an engineer had to deal with the canal company that employed him. Company correspondence and letter books shed much light on the many problems the engineers faced trying to build these stupendous works to budget and on time.

The canal's chief engineer or 'superintendent of works' was responsible for planning its route and designing any major works needed such as bridges, aqueducts or tunnels. A resident engineer was hired to supervise the work on site, as the chief engineer was normally involved with several different projects at once. William Jessop was resident engineer for the Ellesmere Canal, but Telford was the engineer-in-chief.

Engineers' minute books, reports and correspondence have information on the construction and maintenance history for the waterways. New works had to be planned out and the canals and associated buildings kept in good repair. Minutes may include maps and plans or details of properties affected by maintenance work.

As the science of civil engineering progressed, engineers felt it was important to keep in touch with one another and keep abreast of the latest developments. The Institution of Civil Engineers was first founded in 1818; Telford became its first president two years later. The Institution has an archive and library with an important collection of canal engineers' papers, including James Brindley's diaries.

Beech House, Ellesmere. This was Thomas Telford's home while building the Ellesmere Canal.

Telford's elegant cast-iron aqueduct over Chester Road, Nantwich for the Birmingham and Liverpool Junction Canal (now the Shropshire Union).

You can use the NRA index (see Chapter 2) to find engineers' papers. A search of the index for Thomas Telford shows there are over thirty repositories with holdings of Telford records: personal papers, correspondence, reports, plans and other papers. The most important collections can be found in the ICE archives (series T), TNA, TNAS, the National Library of Scotland and the Ironbridge Gorge Museum.

The canal company's secretary, sometimes known as the chief clerk, dealt with the landowners affected by the canal works. He also hired the contractors who cut the canals such as the Pinkerton brothers from Yorkshire. (The chief engineer helped him choose a contractor if necessary.) The Pinkertons worked on several different waterways including the Lancaster Canal and Barnsley Canal.

Canal company minute books, correspondence and letter books will reveal company dealings with contractors and their dissatisfaction if the work had cost over-runs or contractors proved unreliable.

The contractors in their turn hired the labourers and navvies needed to do the hard physical graft. The men usually worked under a 'butty'

Case Study – (River) Weaver Navigation

An 'Extra Labourers Day Wage Book' for the Weaver Navigation in the summer of 1799 gives the names of additional workmen taken on to make repairs at Anderton Basin. J. Lowe, a 'brick-setter', earned a total of 1s 1d for his work between 28 June and 4 July. Samuel Maddock earned 6s for making mortar between 1 July and 4 July. The labourers were evidently thirsty, because 'Thomas Water's bill for ale' came to 10s 3d when the job was completed (CRO D1361/1).

Nearly half a century later, over forty extra labourers were needed to clean out Pickering's Canal, the Barnton Canal and some sections of the Weaver. The men, who included George Hindley, William Walton and John Clarke, were employed from 24–30 May 1844; wages were 1s 3d per day on average. (CRO D1361/3).

system in which they agreed to do a certain amount of labour for a fixed price. A good wage in the late 1790s was 2s 6d per day. Not all contractors were prepared to pay that much and navvies risked the sack if they complained.

After the canal was completed, an engineer's services were still needed to keep it in good repair. The chief engineer did not necessarily stay on to look after the waterway after construction (William Jessop, who built the Trent Navigation, was an exception).

Canal engineers, whether responsible for building or maintaining the inland waterways, wrote down their expenses for the works. They listed the workers employed, number of days worked and wages paid. Labourers and navvies may also be listed in foremen's day wage books. Workers' addresses will not necessarily be included. Day wage books and similar items may be found at local record offices, e.g. Stafford Record Office has Brindley's day books (Mf 79).

James Brindley wrote down the names of his most trustworthy workers on the Bridgewater Canal in his notebooks. Navvies of the canal and railway age used 'bye-names' or nicknames, and one of Brindley's foremen most 'employed on difficult matters' was 'Black David'. Two other workmen whose names popped up frequently were 'Bill o'Tom's' and 'Busick Jack'.

The first navvies were most likely farm labourers recruited locally, or drawn in from other counties as word spread that work was available. As they gained experience, they moved on to other engineering works. Some came from the Lincolnshire fens, the Midlands and northern England. Later navvies were of Scottish and Irish descent.

Navvies were men of legend, notorious not only for their capacity to shovel tons of earth but also for their huge appetites and fist fights – even riots. Working conditions on site were harsh and dangerous and many navvies were killed or injured. Tunnelling was particularly hazardous. The navvies' living accommodation was primitive; perhaps just makeshift turf hovels. The truck system (where food and other necessities were bought from the contractor) was rife.

The great age of canal building had ended by the time of the first censuses for which we have surviving enumerators' schedules (1841 and later) but there are census entries for navvies associated with canal companies, because they were still needed for maintenance work. If using online family history censuses, try searches for 'canal labourer', 'canal navvy', 'excavator,' 'navvy' or 'labourer on canal'.

A search on www.thegenealogist.co.uk (and similar sites) will find families such as William Badrick (49) and his son Ernest (27) listed in the 1901 census as canal labourers at Tring at the Wendover branch of the Grand Junction Canal (RG13/1331). Some labourers had permanent addresses, perhaps if they did regular maintenance work, but some will be found in lodging houses, or just 'by the canal' or 'canal side'.

Many different workers were needed to keep everything running smoothly on the inland waterways: there were agents, office clerks, wharfingers, maintenance men, lockkeepers, toll collectors, office cleaners and even mole catchers.

Wharfingers were responsible for overseeing the canal wharves and warehouses where goods were loaded and unloaded. (This task was not necessarily done by the boatmen and families. Boats on Shropshire Union canal business were unloaded and loaded by the wharfingers and their labourers.) The wharfingers lived in a canal company house (sometimes a substantial building) and received a pension. Wharfingers sometimes also acted as canal agents; some ran their own carrying business and owned boats.

The canal agent in effect wore 'several hats'. Another name for the canal agent was 'superintendent'. He was in overall charge of the wharves where cargoes were loaded and unloaded. He dealt with customers and their complaints. In the early days of the canals, it was his job to maintain discipline and crack down on any trouble with the boatmen, particularly if they had a dust-up over whose turn it was to unload their boat.

Canal companies had their own wharves, which were open to carriers for their use, like those owned by the Leeds and Liverpool Canal Co. Some carriers such as Fellows, Morton & Clayton hired wharfs from the canal company.

Myles Pennington was 'connected with the canal carrying trade from a boy of fourteen, and for many years afterwards'. Myles, who was born at Lancaster on 13 May 1814, later wrote an account of his early life. His father was the agent for canal carrier John Hargreaves, who we met in Chapter 2.

Unlike many boatmen, Myles went to school and learned to read and write. His father set Myles to work in his office when he was still a 'small boy'. Myles wrote out goods invoices for Pennington senior.

In May 1830, when he was 16 years old, Myles went to Preston to start as an apprentice clerk in Hargreaves's fly-boat office. His apprenticeship term was for five years, and his 'wages' were his clothes, bed and board and petty expenditure. After a while he rebelled against having to account for every last penny he spent, and persuaded Hargreaves to give him a weekly wage of 16s instead.

Myles's father and other agents kept cash books in which they noted down the cost of each shipment, wages paid, cash in hand, etc., and calculated the balance each week. A copy of the balance and the original goods invoices were sent to Hargreaves's house at Hart Common, Wigan.

Hargreaves believed in 'hands-on' management. He sent his agents a list of errors once a quarter, and woe betide any agents who owed him money. Mr Hargreaves visited his offices between Manchester and Edinburgh every three months and collected the largest freight accounts so he could check them personally. He was on first-name terms with all his workers

As noted earlier, some boatmen were partial to liquid refreshment, and land workers enjoyed a drink, too. One dark night in 1830, young Myles Pennington discovered all the men at Hargreaves's Preston office (including the agents) were completely sozzled. A train of waggons loaded with butter and other fresh produce for the Manchester market needed taking down the tramroad to Walton Summit, where a canal boat was waiting for the cargo, but the men were in no fit state to travel.

Myles sprang into action and harnessed a team of horses. After an anxious moment when the waggons came off the rails and he had to wake up a nearby farmer to help them get back on track, he got the waggons safely to the canal boat. The plucky lad was 'greeted with three cheers by the boatmen' when he arrived with their cargo.

Canal-company agents are frequently listed in trade directories. Pigot's 1822 *Commercial Directory for Cheshire* lists Robert Bayley as 'agent to the Stafford Canal Co.' at Runcorn. At Altrincham, the agent for the Bridgewater Canal Trustees was Thomas Bayley at Canal Warehouse.

Next in the line of command below the agent was the accountant or 'clerk accountant'. He was responsible for supervising the toll collectors, seeing their books were in order and collecting the tolls from them. If a canal carrier had a tolls account on credit, he collected the money they owed. The accountants in their turn had clerks and book-keepers under them to help ensure the accounts were in order.

Edward Paget-Tomlinson's *Illustrated History of Canal & River Navigations* (Landmark Countryside Collection, 2006) has a helpful section on 'Officers and staff to modern times'. It also gives histories for each canal and river navigation, including mergers or takeovers by other canal or railway companies, which will be helpful if you need to research the company owners for the time when your ancestor was an employee.

Several books have been published on researching your railway ancestors which may help you track down canal staff employed by railway firms, including David T. Hawkings' *Railway Ancestors* (History Press, 2008) and Di Drummond's *Tracing Your Railway Ancestors* (Pen & Sword, 2010). There's a family history society devoted to railway ancestors (www.railwayancestors.org.uk) which publishes CD-ROMs of staff lists.

Case Study

The Shropshire Union Railway and Canal Co. staff register (RAIL 623/67 at TNA) lists several employees, including E.H. Neatherway (canal agent at Burslem on the Trent & Mersey where SURCC had a wharf). Neatherway contributed to the London and North Western Railway Superannuation Fund.

Over time, the administrative staffing arrangements for each waterway became increasingly complex, particularly during the railway age. There were many different tiers of management. In cases where a canal company was leased by a railway firm they might 'share' staff. Office canal staff may be listed under 'traffic staff', with canal wharves listed as 'stations'. A person might be working for a canal company but making payments into a railway company's pension fund.

Canal companies' income was chiefly derived from the tolls they collected. When a boat passed from one company's waterway to another's, it paid a toll even if it was not carrying any cargo. The amount of toll paid depended on the quantity of cargo carried, although some cargoes such as lime or manure were toll-free. To save time, and to avoid the boatmen having to carry money, some carriers had an account on credit with canal companies.

The toll collector or toll clerk had a very important job. He was responsible for checking how much cargo was on board each boat. The boatman carried a toll ticket which showed the type of cargo and quantity, but obviously canal companies wanted to ensure they were not being short-changed. This was calculated by 'gauging' the boat.

The heavier the cargo, the deeper the boat lay in the water. Each boat was 'calibrated' by the canal carrying company at its own expense in an 'indexing' or 'gauging dock' before the boat began its working life.

A different system was used on some other canals. Huge weighing machines weighed the whole boat and its load (the boat was originally weighed empty and a record kept, as for gauging). A nineteenth-century weighing machine which was in service for many decades on the Glamorganshire Canal can be seen at the Stoke Bruerne Canal Museum.

Case Study

The BCN gauging register for 1925 has a sheet for Fellows, Morton & Clayton boat *Camel* gauged at Tipton on 12 February 1925. The boat's FMC fleet number was 291, and its BCN gauge number was 1013 (TWA GD BW165/7/4/42).

This canal-boat weighing machine at Stoke Bruerne Canal Museum was in use on the Glamorganshire Canal until c.1914.

The boat was weighed empty and then repeatedly weighed again with different loads. In each instance a note was made of how much boat was visible above the waterline (the 'freeboard' or 'dry inches'). The boat hull was then clearly marked with gauging index 'strips' so that when the boat arrived at a toll station, all the toll collector had to do was read off the tonnage according to which indexes were visible.

In later years a more complicated method of gauging was used. First the boat was weighed with successively heavier loads at a gauging dock as before. A table or register of measurements was drawn up and a copy kept at each toll house.

When the boat arrived at the toll house, the toll collector gauged it by measuring the freeboard precisely at several points around the boat. The measurement was taken with a rod.

A traveller on the new 'steam fly-boat *Pioneer*' from City Basin on the Grand Junction Canal to Paddington 'had the pleasure of seeing the cargo weighed by a very simple process. The weight of the boat being previously ascertained, all that the gauger has to do is to find, by a long measuring rod, the depth from her waterline to her keel; and a calculation by figures will then enable him to tell the exact weight of the cargo to a fraction' (*Chambers's Journal*, 9 February 1861).

Sometimes the toll collector used a special instrument with a floating marker instead of a rod. The collector then calculated the average reading, and consulted the gauging table. Now he could estimate the cargo weight which corresponded to that number of 'dry inches' and could calculate the toll required.

To save time and costs, a number of companies pooled their resources (as on the River Trent and associated waterways in the late 1790s) and adopted a joint gauging system.

The Birmingham Canal Navigation Co. (BCN) gauged its boats and those of other firms at Smethwick and Tipton. A number of BCN gauging registers exist. Section A3 has information on the location of gauging records.

Some toll stations on very busy navigations like the BCN were in the middle of the canal, which narrowed so that boats were effectively 'funnelled' towards the station.

Toll collectors did not always see eye to eye with the boatmen, who sometimes felt they were being held up unnecessarily and threatened them.

Lock keepers sometimes acted as toll collectors and boat gaugers, too. The main job for lock keepers, though, was to see that the boatmen got quickly through the lock, protect the locks and ensure the boatmen did not waste water or damage lock gates.

On at least one canal (the Birmingham and Liverpool Junction in the 1830s), the company took on labourers who had helped build the canal as lock keepers if they proved hard-working and trustworthy.

In the late eighteenth and early nineteenth centuries, canal staff such as clerks and lock keepers were not immune to temptation if a particularly tasty cargo came their way, and you may find records of prosecutions or disciplinary action by the canal company.

To help reduce pilfering from boats, some canal companies employed watchmen. Joseph Hemingway recorded the 'wilful murder' of a watchman named Boulton on 7 January 1807. He 'was found drowned in the canal locks at Tower Wharf in Chester'.

After 1840 the canal companies had powers to employ their own police to reduce theft and keep a lid on any trouble at the toll houses or locks. You may find these listed in the censuses as 'canal police constable' or 'canal policeman'.

Lock keepers occasionally earned extra money as watchmen, although George Dean, a lock keeper at Wheelock for the NSR, evidently felt he was not paid enough. He earned 3s 4d per day, had a company cottage and earned an additional 3s 2d per day as a watchman. He left the NSR in April 1916 to 'get better wages' elsewhere.

Lock keeping was often taken up by boatmen who were too old to work the boats any longer. If the lure of the canal proved too strong, they returned to the boats as tug-men or dredger-men (less regular work), or worked in canal maintenance yards. Dredgers cleaned out the canal channel to keep it navigable.

Canal companies employed lengthsmen, also known as bank 'rangers' or 'bank walkers'. They were responsible for checking the canal banks were still intact, maintaining the towpaths and cutting back weeds.

Mole catchers worked for canal companies, too. Mole or rabbit activity could wreak havoc with earth embankments and cause a canal breach.

Another canal occupation you may come across is 'horse marine'. On many canals boatmen provided their own horse, but in some places (Yorkshire in particular) horses were hired. These contractors were called 'horse marines'. In Scotland, the men who supplied horses were called 'trackers' and the tracker drove the horse as it towed the boat. In Ireland men doing this job were known as 'haulers'.

Canal companies employed a large number of skilled craftsmen who served apprenticeships such as carpenters, masons, blacksmiths and so on. Canal properties needed maintenance as well as the 'nuts and bolts' of the network: lock gates, bridges, aqueducts and so on.

Samuel Smiles recorded that the skilled workers employed by the Duke of Bridgewater were known locally as 'cunning men'. These men

Lengthsman's hut, old Chester Canal, now the Shropshire Union.

had a fount of practical knowledge but they were superstitious. The 'foreman bricklayer ... ruled the planets' (cast a horoscope) before each new project to check which was the luckiest day to begin work on.

Odd jobs at the maintenance yards were done by unskilled workers. A canal-company house was customary for skilled craftsmen and labourers, and communities of skilled workers grew up by the canal yards.

Runcorn was formerly a tiny village but its population greatly increased after the Bridgewater Canal's construction. Pigot's *Commercial Directory for Cheshire* (1822–1823) noted that 'Many dwelling places, shops, inns, etc.' were built for the 'numerous workmen and other persons attending the vast basons [*sic*] or reservoirs which supply the canal'.

The canals closed for repairs for a few days every summer. This was a very busy time for maintenance workers. Repairing and cleaning out locks was very hard, dirty, muddy work and accidents were not unknown. A foreman or 'ganger' (who reported to the canal engineer) oversaw the work. Major damage to the canal banks such as a breach caused by a landslip or floodwaters meant the men worked round the clock to make repairs because the company could not earn any income until the waterway reopened.

The canal companies employed blacksmiths who were needed to make iron parts for canal lock gates and other lock equipment, as well as shoeing horses. Janet Lane's grandfather Enoch Mason and his father Joseph worked on the nationalized waterways. Enoch Mason lived in Lock House 83, situated by lock 10 at Perry Barr on the Tame Valley Canal.

Janet's mother Florence grew up in the lock house which had a workshop and forge attached: 'Grandad used to shoe the horses in the blacksmith's at the front of the cottage, and I remember pumping the bellows to heat the fire'. Enoch also worked in the pumping station at Deykin Avenue, Aston, where he polished 'every bit of brasswork in the building'.

Canal companies found a house for faithful, long-serving employees when they became too old to work. When Janet's grandparents retired, British Waterways moved them 'to a lovely new dormer bungalow' by the canal, but they died shortly afterwards. 'It was such an upheaval at that late stage in their lives'.

When the canals froze in the depth of winter, gangs of men were employed as ice-breakers. They stood on an 'ice boat' (with an iron hull) which they 'rocked' from side to side until the ice gave way under the boat. The men hung onto a chain or pole in the middle of the boat while they worked. The ice-boat was dragged along the canal by teams of horses to clear a passage for vessels. Ice-breaking was a dangerous job, as the men might fall into the freezing water and drown.

Steam tugs were used as ice-breakers in the later days of the canal era. In addition to his other work Enoch Mason 'worked the ice boats, cutting through the ice on the canals in front of the long boats', Janet Lane recalled. Her mother told her how in wintertime she had to 'help her dad when the carthorses slipped on the iced towpaths into the canal, slipping a rope around their necks and a plank under the belly of the horse to try and haul them to the side. She said they had to get them out quickly before they went wild'.

Carriers usually bought boats ready-made, although some companies such as the Duke of Bridgewater's built their own boats. Boats were needed on the new canals even before the waterway was finished. As soon as one stretch of canal opened, the canal company used it to save transport costs for materials and speed up the rest of the work. When the Bridgewater Canal was under construction, barges were used to carry timber and foundation stones, and one barge contained a smith's forge. Canal companies often had their own boat maintenance yard even if they did not build their own boats.

Famous boat builders include William Nurser at Braunston (narrow boats) from the 1870s onwards, Braithwaite & Kirk at West Bromwich (who built boats for Fellows, Morton & Clayton) and W.J. Yarwood's at Northwich.

You can use the NRA index to find records for boat builders, too. For example, an NRA search for Isaac Pimblott & Co. (which built boats for British Waterways and the Leeds and Liverpool Canal, among other firms) shows that Cheshire Archives hold two sets of records including vessel registers (DDX 435, 524).

Canal-company correspondence and other records may include names of boat builders. Fleet lists (sometimes called boat registers) such as the Leeds and Liverpool Canal Company register for the early 1950s record each boat's name, when and where built, the constructor's name and maintenance details (Gloucester Docks waterways archive).

Boat builders' financial records and correspondence may show payments to staff. The names of boat builders or boat-building firms are often shown on gauging tables.

Boat builders, like other skilled craftsmen, served apprenticeships and these may be detailed in company records.

Case Study

The staff ledger of the Canals Department of the North Staffordshire Railway (NSR) for 1850–1930 has some fascinating records of workers. The ledger includes personal details such as dates of birth and deaths as well as wages and pension payments.

Joseph Gripton began his working life as a labourer for the NSR on 18 November 1907. Joseph's date of birth was noted as 5 July 1892, and his starting wage was 8s per week. In June 1902 he was promoted to apprentice boat builder, and his wages increased to 10s per week. By December 1912 he was earning 18s per week, but on 15 January 1916 he enlisted in the army.

Joseph survived the war; he left the army on 15 April 1918 (perhaps because he was wounded) and rejoined the company. In 1924 he was promoted again to boat builder earning a princely 42s per week. Six years later, Gripton was transferred to another department and he disappears from the ledger on 6 June 1932 (TWA EPort 20001.146).

Canal-boat builders clustered by the canals, as might be expected, and the censuses for Staffordshire and Lancashire in particular reveal many men with that occupation. Other likely places to find names and addresses for boat-building firms are trade and street directories, advertisements in newspapers and telephone books (from the 1880s).

The *Gloucestershire Directory* (1820) lists John Bird, 'ship and barge builder'. He was 'proprietor of the dry dock on the Gloucester and Berkeley Canal' and his address is given as 'Southgate St'. No house number is given, but houses did not necessarily have a number at this time.

News reports are always worth checking, too. A letter to the editor of *The Times* (14 July 1864) told of one canal-boat family's narrow escape from death thanks to a Wolverhampton boat builder's quick thinking.

In July 1864, the canal boat *Lincolnshire* was on its way from Wolverhampton to Bilston with a cargo of grain. The *Lincolnshire* was a Duke of Bridgewater Trustees boat. Its master was Thomas Whitehouse, who had his wife and three children on board; the eldest child was only 6 years old. As the boat passed Monmore Green, opposite Major's chemical works, the horse towing it trotted to the wrong side of the telegraph poles near the canal. As Whitehouse tried to coax the horse onto the right path, it suddenly broke away and pulled the towing line taut, just as the boat was negotiating a sharp bend in the canal.

The boat was pulled right over so it capsized and was left bottom upwards. Mrs Whitehouse and her children were trapped inside; the cabin was several feet under water.

Boat builder Joseph Monk was working nearby and saw the accident. He sent one of his men to get an axe, raced to the boat and jumped onto the hull. The boat had settled slightly, and a few inches of the cabin were now visible above the water. Monk could hear the mother and her children crying inside, so he knew they were still alive. He hacked his way through the 3in-thick oak timbers until he made an opening.

A child's tiny hand reached out, and Monk redoubled his efforts to widen the gap in the timbers. The more he cut, the more the woman and children tried to get their hands and arms through the hole, which slowed him down.

At last Monk reached inside and grabbed the youngest child, a 10-month-old toddler. With the help of Christopher Horton, a cooper at the chemical works, the mother and her other children were rescued from the stricken boat. The shaken family were taken on board a boat belonging to the chemical works, where they were cared for. The whole rescue took about twenty minutes; the anonymous letter writer felt Monk was a hero, and deserved a medal.

When canal boats went to the maintenance yard to be spruced up, their paintwork was freshened up. There have been many different theories on how the custom of painting canal boats with bright colours and patterns originated, but no one really has a definitive answer.

Hollingshead described the decoration of the fly boat *Stourport* in the late 1850s. The boatmen's 'chosen colours' were 'red, yellow and blue … The two sides of the cabin, seen from the bank and the towing path, present a couple of landscapes, in which there is a lake, a castle, a sailing boat, and a range of mountains.'

A *Birmingham Daily Mail* report quoted in *Our Canal Population* depicted a similar cabin two decades later: 'Any and every article' was decorated by the 'canal boat artist … Inside he rejoices in highly illuminated panels'. The boatman's bucket or pail was adorned with 'designs of outrageous roses and sunflowers' and its base depicted 'a gay cavalier or valiant crusader in full armour'. 'Dazzling' knobs made from china or brass brightened up the cabin.

The wide-beam boat and keels on the northern canals were decorated in a more minor key to their Midland counterparts. On the Leeds and Liverpool Canal, geometric patterns and ornate shapes were favoured, although flowers were used, too.

A family gathering on an unidentified Surrey canal in the 1920s. These boats were owned by the famous carrying firm of Fellows, Morton & Clayton. Cassell's Book of Knowledge (*Waverley Book Co., n.d., c.1924*).

The boats and workers of the Anderton Co. at Stoke-on-Trent were called 'knobsticks' and boat painter William Hodgson's highly individual rose and castle illustrations on Anderton craft in the twentieth century became known as the 'knobstick' style. Herbert Tooley at Banbury and Frank Nurser at Braunston were both well known for their beautiful canal art. Some owner-boatmen painted their own boats and took pride in their work.

When John Brydone was appointed as first Chief Inspector of canal boats in 1884 by the Local Government Board, he became fascinated by the brightly painted boats and the boat families' way of life.

Chapter 6

'BOATER KIDS'

John Brydone faced a massive task as he got to grips with his new job enforcing the new sanitary legislation for canal boats. Brydone rolled up his sleeves and set to work.

Just 3 months into his appointment, he visited 94 registration authorities (there were now 115 in total) from Goole to Gloucester. He travelled over 3,000 miles in total and personally inspected over 600 canal boats.

He was responsible for collating all the information from inspectors on the canal network and sent a yearly report to the board. Brydone's first account appeared in the LGB report for 1884–1885.

He discovered that although over 8,500 boats had been registered before 30 September 1884, 'many boats have been and still are going up and down our canals unregistered'.

Brydone worked tirelessly to improve boat families' living conditions in the face of pettifogging complaints about his work from officials at the Local Government Board. They viewed Brydone's suggestions for improvements to boat cabins and comments on boat life in his reports with deep suspicion. He was not paid to act as a social reformer.

Yet Brydone could not help commenting on waterways life: 'Many of the boatpeople keep their cabins clean and bright, with here and there some suitable illuminated texts displayed, while some have flowers and birds along with them'.

Brydone was surprised by the contrasts he saw among boating families. He noted: 'the cleanest boats were almost invariably those on which there was no woman, but worked entirely by men'.

He felt some children would be better looked after if parents did not spend so much time in the pub. When he visited some keel-men (in the Yorkshire area), one family of six who lived on their boat full-time were in a sorry state: 'The cabin was dirty, the man and his wife no better, and the children worse'. All was 'wretchedness and misery'. When Brydone remonstrated with the captain, he said he could 'do no better; he could scarce make ends meet'.

Yet another keel nearby was 'clean and tidy'. It was worked by 'a man and his wife with their eldest son as mate, and another son assisting him'. The captain kept a house on land for his eleven other children, 'who could all read and write'. Both captains worked for the same company, and earned the same pay. Brydone believed the difference was because the parents on the first boat frittered away their money in the 'beer-shop'.

Brydone found the sanitary authorities were in disarray about how to implement the regulations. Many cabins still had insufficient ventilation. Sometimes the only ventilation provided was a sliding panel over a hole between the cabin and the hold. If the hold was filled with freight, this vent was useless. Other boats had ventilators in the side or roof of the boat, but families 'stuffed up' the holes so they did not feel a draught in the cabin.

Owners did not bother to inform the registration authorities when their boat had a new master (something to bear in mind if you check the registers). Brydone also found boatmen did not keep their certificates on board, because prior to his visit 'it was the first time they had been asked for them or that anyone had inspected their boats'.

Brydone was keen to encourage boatmen to keep a home on land if possible. In February 1895, Brydone made a public appeal for donations for distressed boatmen who had been unable to work for three weeks owing to a sharp frost. In addition to feeding their families, it cost each boatman 12s a week or more to feed and stable his horse. Brydone was worried boatmen who had recently taken houses on shore so they could send their children to school would be tempted back on the boats again to save money.

An edited version of John Brydone's reports can be read in the LGB reports, which are parliamentary papers (see Section A1). His correspondence from 1883 to 1889 is archived at TNA in the LGB series MH 32/94. After Brydone left in 1899, Owen J. Llewellyn was chief inspector of canal boats for over thirty years.

By the beginning of the twentieth century, it was all too clear that the Canal Boats Acts, as educational measures, were dead in the water. A survey of Birmingham canal-boat children found over half of them did not know their alphabet, and only a small proportion of them could read a simple book.

The main problem was that as soon as children were big enough to help on board, their parents took them out of school. In Gloucester in the late 1910s, boatmen's children who lived on land, especially boys, began working on the boats when they were about 8 years old. Boat children just picked up scraps of education wherever they could.

The school boards and their truancy officers faced real problems trying to enforce the legislation. For example in Cheshire, parents pulled the wool over the eyes of school-board officers in Sandbach by telling them their children went to school in Runcorn, and vice versa. The children never went to school at all.

A number of school boards tried to make special provision for boat children. Greenway Road School at Runcorn (later Victoria Road School), founded in 1886, had a special class for boat children and others who had never been to school.

The place where a boat was registered might be miles away from where a boat family regularly worked. Some parents preferred to pay the fines for non-attendance rather than risk losing their children's labour.

Boat children were not always welcomed by teachers in ordinary schools. They were not as advanced as those who attended regularly, so the teacher put them at the back of the class with a primer.

School grants depended on attendance figures, and boat children's irregular attendance played havoc with a school's scoring under the system. Many LEAs simply threw up their hands in despair, declaring it was impossible to educate canal children until they were taken off the boats permanently. While the authorities argued over the best solution, the missions continued working with the boat people.

In the mid-1890s a special school at Brentford was established for boat children by the London City Mission. After a brief period of closure the school moved to the Boatmen's Institute (Brentford) in 1920 and was taken under local education authority control.

The London City Mission was also responsible for the Boatmen's Institute at Paddington which had a school attached (it was taken over by London County Council in the 1930s). The Incorporated Seamen's and Boatmen's Friend Society (ISBSF) ran schools at Sheffield, Leeds and Birmingham.

The Salvation Army took an interest in the boat people. In the 1950s two of their missionaries, Brigadier and Mrs Fielding, travelled on the Midlands' canals on narrow boats and gave pastoral care and practical help in addition to Sunday school lessons.

Trade unions and the National Society for the Prevention of Cruelty to Children (NSPCC) waged a long campaign to get children off canal boats. The NSPCC had long been interested in canal-boat children's welfare.

The *Northwich Guardian* (26 July 1893) reported the society's prosecution for cruelty against John and Ellen Storer from Runcorn for ill-treating 7-year-old Joseph Nash. The Storers worked narrow boats *Ann* and *Job*.

John Storer said the boy had been 'given to him by his mother Annie Nash' in February the previous year. When the NSPCC inspector found Joseph, he was dirty, half-starved and a 'mass of bruises'.

In another distressing case at the turn of the century, a boatman who was reprimanded by the NSPCC inspector about the way he treated his sons was later discovered to have sold them to another boatman. In 1920 the society appointed a special inspector to look after canal-boat children.

The society loudly condemned the canal trade's reliance on child labour. For example, working the locks was extremely hard work and some people felt this was beyond young children's strength, as well as putting them in danger. During the early 1920s, an NSPCC inspector claimed to have witnessed a very young child struggling to work the gate paddles, but it is hard to say if this was an everyday occurrence.

The Transport Workers' Federation also put pressure on the government. The union believed women's and children's working conditions had changed little since the 1870s and they were used as cheap labour. Many

At the windlass, 1870s. A young boatwoman operating lock gates. Drawing by Herbert Johnson for Our Canal Population *(London, 1879).*

boatmen could not afford to keep a house on land for their families unless canal companies and carriers paid higher and more regular wages.

In 1920 the government set up a Departmental Committee on 'Living-In on Canal Boats' which reported the following year. The committee made the first reasonably accurate survey of canal-boat children. It found only 1,200 children under the age of 14 on canal boats, and not all these children lived permanently on board. Approximately 700 children were of school age but few went to school. The committee suggested children should no longer be allowed to live on canal boats during term time, but the government simply ignored this recommendation.

The committee had some positive findings: 'The presence of the wife and mother on board helps to preserve a high standard of morality among the men and a kindly but efficient discipline among the children'.

The Board of Education was not anxious to grasp the nettle regarding canal-boat children's schooling. Little money was available to make special provision for boat children and the number of children living full-time on boats was falling rapidly. In Liverpool, the number of boats registered under the Canal Boats Acts was 607 in 1900; by 1929 the number had fallen to 352 boats.

The board did raise concerns that children's health was being put at risk from noxious cargoes. In the 1920s families with young children lived on boats carrying household and street refuse from Paddington Basin and West Drayton. However, the various government departments involved such as the Ministry of Health 'passed the buck' so successfully that no action was taken to provide better sanitary facilities at the canal wharves or to stop families living on these boats.

Women and children had little protection in law if they became sick or had an accident. They did not count as 'employees' in the eyes of the canal companies because they worked for the boatman, not the company, so they received no compensation if they were injured.

In 1924 this situation changed for families on boats owned by Fellows, Morton & Clayton, and Thomas Clayton of Oldbury. The mates on these boats (usually the boatman's wife) were now classed as company employees, which meant they could claim sick pay or accident compensation. The Grand Union Canal Carrying Company followed suit in the late 1930s, but many other companies left boatwomen to fend for themselves.

Boat families still had only limited access to medical care. Babies were born in boat cabins with little help from doctors or midwives, but somehow the mothers coped remarkably well. The *Midwife* (*British Journal of Nursing Supplement*, 27 August 1921) noted from the Living-In Committee's report that many canal-boat children were born: 'on board the boats under conditions quite unsuitable for mother or child in cases of confinement, yet one nurse with considerable experience of these cases asserted that she had never known of a case where a mother died in confinement, and only one case where a child was born dead'.

The medical authorities were slow to take an interest in boaters and it was not for another two decades that midwives and nurses visited the boats on a more regular basis.

Sister Mary Ward was a real friend in need to boat families. She had a house by the locks at Stoke Bruerne on the Grand Union Canal. Sister Ward gave the boat people free medical care for many decades, most of which was paid for out of her own pocket.

The decline in horse boating in the 1930s as motor boats became more common did not bring a swift end to family boats. In fact a narrow-boat wife and children could now enjoy extra living space, towed behind the motor boat in another boat or 'butty'.

On the wide-beam boats of the northern canals such as the Leeds and Liverpool, however, the new diesel engines swallowed up a great deal of the space formerly used as cabin accommodation, and families began to leave the canals.

Meanwhile, the Transport and General Workers Union (TGWU) and the NSPCC were still fighting to get families off canal boats. These efforts were greatly resented by the boat people, who wanted to keep their traditional way of life intact.

Harry Gosling, the TGWU leader, tried to introduce a Canal Boats bill in 1929. He hoped children under 14 could be removed from the boats by being 'boarded out' at special schools during term time, then allowed back on family boats during school holidays.

This suggestion had been made by reformers in the previous century. An earlier attempt to set up a hostel at Wolverhampton in the late 1880s failed because parents did not want to send their children there. The only place where this idea appears to have worked successfully for a while was at Wood End, Erdington in Birmingham, where a hostel was set up for canal children, but this was not until the 1950s.

However, Gosling's bill raised a storm of protest by MPs and others concerned about the break-up of family life. The missions were appalled by this proposed intrusion into family life. They felt families should stay together. The boaters petitioned Parliament against the bill and it failed.

A notable attempt was made in 1930 to educate canal children while accommodating their families' traditions. On 30 September 1930 *The Times* reported that the Paddington Canal Boatmen's Institute, with the aid of the Grand Union Canal Carrying Co., had set up a 'floating school'.

The barge *Elsdale* was tied up at the Otter Dock, West Drayton on the Grand Union Canal, for which the company charged the Institute a peppercorn rent. Boat children attended classes there when their parents' boats stayed for a few days in the area. *Elsdale* was supervised at first by Captain Thorley of the Church Army, and was used as an elementary day school and Sunday school. Middlesex LEA took over the school shortly after its foundation.

Elsdale moved to Bulls Bridge in 1939. After an unfortunate incident (it sank!) the boat was no longer considered canal-worthy and moved onto the land. It was hoped the new location would make it more accessible to boat children and class sizes would increase: Bulls Bridge was the Grand Union's biggest dockyard and a very busy canal junction. From this date the Heston and Isleworth Education Committee took over the running of the school.

As the amount of work available on the canals declined during the twentieth century, parents grew increasingly worried their children would not be able to get jobs on the land if they could not read or write. Old attitudes to education died hard, however.

Lily Wakefield was taken out of school so she could help her parents: 'I was on the point of reading when they took me away at about six years old to go on the boat'. She did not get enough 'schooling to write a letter' and never saw a school inspector: 'No-one ever checked' to see if Lily went to school.

But Lily had some 'lovely memories … I opened gates for the horse while going along the River Weaver. My dad used to go ahead to get the locks ready. It was lovely when it was summer, picking buttercups.'

Kenneth Wakefield went to school until he was about 9 years old, when: 'I came back to the canal. I went back on the boat to help because my brother wanted a boat of his own.'

Unlike many boat people, Ken had learned to read and write. To help them out, the missions and friendly societies wrote letters for boaters when needed. The lock keepers and toll collectors, too, would read boat people's post for them and deal with correspondence.

Gladys Horne (daughter of Edward Price) was born on an FMC boat at Birmingham in the early 1930s. She did not get the chance to learn to read and write. She courted her future husband Sam Horne with the help of friendly lock keepers, who read Gladys's letters from Sam to her, and wrote back on her behalf. Later, when Gladys and Sam left the boats for a home on land, she went to night school.

The issue of canal-boat children's education only died with the end of commercial carrying with narrow boats during the 1960s. School registers may record boat children as they passed through a particular district. School Board records after 1877 (following the Canal Boats Acts) may have information on arrangements for canal children. Reports from the Board of Education (series ED at TNA) also mention boat children.

Balfour's Education Act of 1902 abolished school boards in December of that year. New local education authorities were set up to control primary and secondary education, and their records should be located at your local county archive.

Wendy Freer's *Women and Children of the Cut* (Railway and Canal Historical Society, 1995) takes a detailed look at children's education and living conditions. Freer has shown the number of canal boatmen in England reached its zenith some time in the 1850s and declined steadily overall after that. One or two regions briefly bucked the trend. The

The rivals: canal, road and railway transport criss-cross at Stanley Dock on the Leeds and Liverpool Canal in the 1890s. Our Railways, Vol. I (Cassell & Co., 1896).

Manchester Ship Canal increased trade in north-west England. Staffordshire boatmen enjoyed a period of prosperity as demand for coal and iron rose, and the Paddington and Brentford areas of the Grand Junction Canal were kept busy. But between the early 1910s and the early 1950s, numbers of workers fell sharply in all areas.

The canals were still losing freight to the railways. There were too many boatmen and not enough work to go round. The Royal Commission on Canals and Inland Navigations was set up in 1906 to look into the freight wars. It confirmed that railways now controlled the lion's share of Britain's freight. On just one railway (the Great Western) more tonnage of freight was carried than the total carried by whole of Britain's waterways.

The Commission found that the lack of centralized control over the waterways created difficulties. Early in the twentieth century, a canal carrier who wanted to send goods from Liverpool to London, say, faced paying tolls to nine or more different canal companies depending on the route taken.

The Commission recommended that the government should subsidize the modernization of the waterways network. Main routes should be widened so vessel sizes could be increased, and the number of locks on some waterways reduced. The political upheavals of the early twentieth century meant that Britain's waterways were seen by the government as a low priority.

The First World War changed the lives of millions and had a huge impact on the inland waterways, too. Britain's trade and industry were inevitably disrupted. The government took over the railways and those canals under railway ownership, but independent canal operators were left out in the cold. Firms such as Fellows, Morton & Clayton could not run their boats profitably because the government had fixed freight prices. When the Canal Control Committee of 1917 was set up to improve the transport of supplies, more carriers were taken over, but canal workers' wages lagged behind those of railway workers.

Many brave boaters fought for Britain and died in the trenches. Some of those who survived, and who had a fresh outlook on life after their ordeal, did not return to the canals. Other boatmen who served their country as munitions workers or in other protected occupations found they could earn higher and more regular wages away from the cut, even though boatmen's wages went up during the war years.

As a result, canal companies struggled to crew their boats and after the war the drift away from the waterways became a torrent.

The Canal Control Committee established a forty-eight hour working week for all canal boatmen in 1919, but as this would have impacted adversely on narrow boatmen's wages, they had their pay raised by one-third to compensate. Government ownership of independent canals ended the following year.

In the previous century, canal boatmen were not noted for their militancy despite long working hours. This was because they lived in 'tied' accommodation (unless they owned their own boat). If they complained too loudly to the canal company about pay and conditions, they lost their home as well as their job. Nevertheless, they took action when they felt aggrieved: there were strikes in the 1890s on the Rochdale Canal, Regent's Canal and other waterways.

There were a number of boatmen's unions at that time. The Royal Commission on Labour (1892) mentions the Watermen and Riverside Labourers' Union, the Dock, Wharf, Riverside and General Labourers' Union and others.

The National Transport Workers' Federation (NTF) tried to improve conditions for boatmen during the First World War. The industrial unrest of the early 1920s prompted many canal boatmen to join the Transport and General Workers Union (TGWU). Section A2 has information on union records.

Another indicator that wages for boatmen were not very attractive is that fewer young men joined the boats in the early decades of the twentieth century. Wages were an increasingly emotive issue, however, and matters came to a head with a famous strike in 1923.

After the First World War, Fellows, Morton & Clayton was in financial difficulty because of the war years. Its boatmen were asked to accept a pay cut. The TGWU called for strike action, and FMC boatmen blockaded the canal at Braunston with their boats. The strike lasted for over twelve weeks before agreement was reached.

As the big operators abandoned the canals after the First World War, the number of owner-boatmen grew briefly. Some were boatmen who had been sacked when the carriers closed. They snapped up the boats being sold off cheaply and set up their own businesses. There was still some life left in the canal carrying trade.

But this proved a false dawn. The 'Number Ones' declined again as yet more freight left the canals. Owner-boatmen such as Harry King, who worked on the Grand Junction Canal and other waterways, sold off their boats and got colliery or other work. As unemployment grew, life on the land beckoned. Fewer than 10 per cent of boatmen were 'Number Ones' in the early 1930s.

The advent of the Second World War brought more change to the canals. Once again the canals were needed to keep Britain's industry moving, and once again there was a shortage of boat crews. Women such as Margaret Cornish, Susan Woolfit and others who had never worked on the canals stepped into the breach and became trainee boatwomen.

They were dubbed 'idle women' by the boaters because of the 'I W' badges they wore (short for Inland Waterways). The lessons of the First World War were not learned and it was not until 1942 that the most vital waterways and carriers were brought under government control.

The canals suffered from bomb damage during the war; the Liverpool area was particularly badly affected. Some sections of canals were forced to close. The industry was once again under-funded by the government. Canal companies could not afford maintenance work and the infrastructure deteriorated from neglect as well as the unwelcome attention of enemy bombers. More carriers threw in the towel after the war as more freight left the waterways.

The Transport Act of 1947, which came into force on 1 January 1948, nationalized the canal network. Over 2,000 miles of canals were now controlled by the British Transport Commission (BTC) which administered the rail network and some road haulage. However, not all canals and rivers were included in the nationalized network. The Manchester Ship Canal, the Bridgewater Canal and others, the River Thames and river navigations were excluded.

The Docks & Inland Waterways Executive (DIWE), which was part of the BTC, took over the responsibility for the nationalized waterways network. Independent carriers such as Fellows, Morton & Clayton were not nationalized, although FMC sold its fleet to DIWE when it gave up carrying in 1949.

The DIWE was abolished by the Transport Act of 1953 and replaced by British Transport Waterways, which officially took over the inland waterways network for England and Wales at the beginning of 1955. It no longer had a docks department. In the 1960s British Transport Waterways phased out carrying in the Midlands and on the Leeds and Liverpool Canal and concentrated on broad waterways such as the Aire & Calder.

In the Irish Republic it took some time for the canal network to come completely under state control (1949). In Northern Ireland canals were still privately owned, but traffic was in decline and they were closed by 1954. In Scotland and in Wales, many canals had closed and there was only a very limited traffic left by the 1950s.

The canal network was increasingly viewed by the authorities as a relic of a bygone age. The national transport system was dominated by rail and increasingly by road haulage. There seemed little point spending money on improvements, and it seemed as if the canals were doomed. Some were filled in because they were too costly to maintain. Others were simply abandoned, with only the bleached timbers of a decaying boat to show water once flowed there.

When L.T.C. Rolt undertook his landmark voyage in narrow boat *Cressy* early in 1939, he met some of the last boating families at work on the Oxford Canal, including Joseph Skinner and the Hone family. After the war he returned to the canals and was saddened to find the number

A scene on an unidentified North Wales canal near the Berwyn mountains (probably the Llangollen Canal) in the 1920s. Cassell's Book of Knowledge (*Waverley Book Co., n.d., c.1924*).

of owner-boatmen had declined even further. The canals were neglected, choked with weeds and mud and freight once carried by water was now taken by lorry.

Rolt's book *Narrow Boat* was published in 1944. Its idyllic, nostalgic picture of the boating life that was fast disappearing inspired a movement to save Britain's neglected canals. The Inland Waterways Association (IWA) was founded two years later by Rolt, Charles Hadfield, Robert Aickman and Frank Eyre. The IWA fought not only to save the canal network but to restore the canals that had been lost or neglected. An IWA for Ireland was formed in 1954.

The appearance of pleasure craft in the early 1950s pointed to a possible new source of income for the waterways but officialdom was slow to respond. More and more canals were threatened with closure as they fell into disrepair and became un-navigable.

Improvements were made on some commercial waterways after Lord Rusholme's survey for the BTC recommended additional investment. Waterways that had become important for pleasure craft were left facing an uncertain future, however, and public disquiet led to another official enquiry. The Bowes Committee of 1956 recommended retaining some canals for freight and recreation and the closure of some stretches of waterway. Tolls should be abolished on some waterways and a system of licences for boats introduced instead.

The birth of the motorway network in the late 1950s made road haulage even more profitable and accelerated the canal carrying trade's decline. In 1963, the newly formed British Waterways Board took over the network after the BTC was disbanded by the government. As commercial carrying on the narrow waterways became less and less profitable, in the early 1960s British Waterways concentrated its efforts instead on wide navigations such as the Aire & Calder and the River Trent.

Some firms such as the Mersey, Weaver & Ship Canal Carrying Co. switched to motor boats, but horses were still used as motive power surprisingly late in the twentieth century. On the Lancaster Canal, horse-drawn boats were used until 1960. Tom Pudding boats carried coal on the Aire & Calder until the late 1960s.

There was still some narrow-boat traffic. The Willow Wren company took over some of British Waterways' narrow boats when it abandoned that arm of its fleet in 1963 after an exceptionally harsh winter. Willow Wren carried grain on horse-drawn boats from mills on the River Nene to Wellingborough until 1969. When the company's narrow-boat freight drew to a close that year, it marked the end of the way of life begun by Brindley's Grand Trunk Canal almost two centuries earlier.

British Waterways stopped carrying freight in 1987 but some specialist, preservation and volunteer boats have kept the tradition alive. The growth of the pleasure-boat industry has brought new life to the canals, too. The tireless efforts of preservation groups have re-opened derelict canals such as the Ashton in north-west England.

Wonders of a bygone age such as the Anderton Boat Lift in Cheshire have been restored and new engineering marvels like the Falkirk Wheel in Scotland have replaced some of the broken 'links' in Britain's waterways.

The story of Britain's inland waterways is still unfolding. At the time of writing plans are afoot for a new 'national trust' for waterways in England and Wales. There are proposals to turn British Waterways into a charitable trust.

Yet many tales from the past have yet to be told: those of the people who worked on the waterways long ago. It is hoped this book will help you begin your own voyage of discovery.

The Anderton Boat Lift at Cheshire after restoration.

A
STARTING YOUR RESEARCH

FAMILY HISTORY BASICS, CENSUSES AND MORE

If one of your ancestors lived or worked on the canals, you may feel daunted by the task ahead. Fortunately, more and more family history resources are becoming available all the time. Tracking down ancestors who were constantly on the move isn't always easy, but gallons of archive material are available to help narrow down your search.

Your family history research begins at home. Ask relatives and friends for information and gather as many hard facts as you can – dates, family names, copies of birth, marriage and death certificates, old photographs, mourning cards – anything that will help to build up your family tree. Oral histories are invaluable but not always reliable sources because relatives' memories may be inaccurate for events that happened many years ago.

It can save time searching if you have a home computer but it is not essential to have your own if cost is an issue. You can book time for free on a computer at a public library.

Keep accurate records and file them in an organized manner so you can easily retrieve the facts you have discovered. Whenever possible, check names and dates against other sources to help verify the accuracy of your family tree.

The key dates for genealogists are the beginning of compulsory civil registration of births, marriages and deaths: England and Wales (1837), Scotland (1855) and Ireland (1864).

Birth certificates show the date and location of the person's birth, name, sex, father's name, mother's maiden name and residence, father's occupation, the date when the birth was registered and the name and address of the person who registered the birth.

Marriage certificates give the date when the couple married, the place where the marriage was solemnized, the name and occupation of the bride and groom, their residence at the time of marriage and the name and occupation of the bride's and groom's father. The witnesses to the marriage may be relatives of the couple.

Death certificates give the person's age and occupation, date of death and residence at the time of death, cause of death, the date when the death was registered and the name and address of the person who registered the death.

Indexes are available for birth, marriage and death certificates; there are copies of the indexes at some main libraries, record offices and online. Each year is divided into quarters for the index. You can use the index reference to order copies of certificates from the appropriate General Register Office for your ancestor's country of origin.

For the era prior to civil registration, you will need to look for parish registers. Parishes began keeping registers of baptisms, marriages and deaths from the 1530s onwards, although there are gaps in the records, especially during the Civil War and Interregnum (c.1640–1660). Remember that the baptism of a child might have taken place several weeks or even months after its birth, so a baptismal record can give only a very rough guide to an ancestor's birth date.

Parish registers for England and Wales which are over a hundred years old but not currently in use are archived with diocesan records at your local record office. Some record offices and genealogy websites have put transcripts of parish registers online with searchable databases. Copies of parish registers are available to buy online from family history societies or on CD-ROM.

If you are having trouble finding a parish record for your ancestor, perhaps because the original register is missing, incomplete or illegible, check if bishops' transcripts are available for the parish in question. In England and Wales, copies of parish registers were sent every year to the church authorities. Bishops' transcripts, however, like any other record, may be subject to copying errors or missing entries. Copies are usually kept at county archives (a few are held by specialist repositories such as university libraries). In general, parishes ceased making bishops' transcripts when civil registration was introduced in 1837.

When looking for parish registers for boat families, think of the routes along which they travelled as their home 'parish'. For example, Braunston was a popular place for boaters' weddings in Northamptonshire: All Saints' Church was known locally as the 'Boaters' Cathedral' and many boatmen and boatwomen are buried there. Tipton and Deritend were also favourite stopping places in the Midlands.

Many boat people were looked down on by society and were not always welcomed by the established church, so you should also check

Nonconformist records and non-parochial registers. From 1753 until the beginning of civil registration, Methodists and other dissenters had to marry in Anglican churches (you may find references to 'Anabaptists'). Quakers and Jews were exempt from this requirement.

Nonconformist registers are kept at the General Register Office for each country. TNA's collection can be searched online at www.bmdregisters.co.uk and many local record offices have copies.

Cemetery records, burial registers and monumental inscriptions can supply information on family members not recorded elsewhere. Many family history societies have compiled transcriptions of these and a National Burial Index is available on CD-ROM from the Federation of Family history Societies.

Wills and probate grants can 'fill in the gaps' before civil registration and between the decennial censuses. If your ancestor owned a boat or part-share in a boat, or owned a boat-building firm, or had canal company shares, then these items may be mentioned in their will. Wills (mostly before c.1750) sometimes included an inventory of the deceased's property and belongings.

Before 1858 (when the Probate Act of 1857 came into force) wills had to be 'proved' (i.e. the will was confirmed as valid and probate granted) in local church courts. Wills and probate grants prior to this date are usually kept at your local record office. Indexes are available online, at the Society of Genealogists' library and on CD-ROM.

After 1858 wills were proved at local civil probate registries which sent copies to the Principal Probate Registry (now the Principal Registry of the Family Division). Copies can be ordered by post from York Probate Sub-Registry.

County record offices normally have microfilm copies of wills proved in local probate offices. Original wills after 1858 (for England and Wales) can be viewed at the Probate Search Room in London. From 1858 registers were kept of estates liable for death duties (only estates worth over £20 or more), and indexes and some registers on microfilm are available at TNA.

The National Library of Wales has microfilm copies of some 500 Welsh parish registers, non-parochial registers and a large collection of bishops' transcripts. Images of wills before 1858 can be viewed for free on the library's website.

For Scotland, indexes of old parish registers and wills and testaments can be searched online at the ScotlandsPeople website. There are no bishops' transcripts for Scottish parishes.

For Ireland, in many cases parish registers are kept at the original parishes. Microfilm copies of Roman Catholic parish registers are held at the National Library of Ireland. Church of Ireland parish registers for the north of Ireland are kept at the Public Record Office of Northern Ireland (PRONI). Copies of Church of Ireland parish registers can be viewed at the Representative Church Body Library in Dublin.

The International Genealogical Index (IGI) is an index of baptism, marriage and death records created by the Church of Jesus Christ of Latter-Day Saints. Copies should be available at your local record office, but entries should always be checked against the original records where possible.

The index can be searched online: www.familysearch.org/eng/default.asp and https://beta.familysearch.org.

Censuses

The first national census of Britain's population was taken in 1801 and thereafter a fresh census was undertaken every ten years. The first censuses were just a head count for statistics. A few small local censuses were made by parish overseers and other officials, and publications on these are available including the Federation of Family History Societies' guide by J. Gibson and M.T. Medlycott, *Local census listings, 1522–1930: holdings in the British Isles* (Birmingham, 1997).

It was not until the 1841 census that data on individuals was collected nationally. This census included details of householders but listings were fairly basic: the place where the census was taken, the address, name (forename and surname only), sex and occupation of the inhabitants of each household and whether the person(s) were born in or out of the county, or outside England. People born in Scotland were designated by a letter 'S', Ireland by 'I' and people from overseas by 'F' (foreign).

The ages of each member of the family over 15 years of age were rounded down in five-year 'steps', so that a 21-year-old, say, was listed as age 20. Enumerators did not have to include the occupation of a worker's wife or child employed by him. This means a boatman's wife's and children's occupations was not mentioned even if they worked on the boat.

It appears only a haphazard effort was made to create complete 'household' listings for boats on the inland waterways in the 1841 or the following census. Some canal companies were asked to estimate how many people lived on their boats. However, some 1841 census schedules do include canal boats. For example, the Brooks family and Terry family are among those listed living in canal boats tied up at Stourbridge Wharf in the hamlet of Amblecote, Staffordshire.

For the 1851 census more detail was collected on each individual. Middle names were included (sometimes just initials), their age, occupation, county and birth parish (for England and Wales) or country of birth (if outside England and Wales).

In this census (and successive ones) special schedules were used for merchant vessels. These schedules listed the name of boat, registration number and tonnage as well as names of the master and crew.

In 1861 local census officials were asked to enquire where canal boats were likely to be tied up. On census day an enumerator was sent to the wharves, canal basins and towpaths to collect information, where he filled in a ship's schedule for each craft. Only boats that were in the area shortly before census day were enumerated; boats that turned up on census day were not included, and this may account for the elusiveness of some boat families. Ship's schedules were not apparently widely used for canal craft for this or the previous census; they may have not survived.

The 1871 census required captains or masters of vessels to fill in the special ship's schedules. These were collected by the enumerator on the morning after census night and used to complete the census return, and these schedules should be found after the household returns for that location. If the original household schedule has survived then you may be able to see your ancestor's handwriting.

In 1881 boats that arrived in a canal-side area or dock on the morning of the census were included in the schedules for the first time.

The 1911 census was the first one for which the original returns completed by each householder were kept. This census collected additional information on families (e.g. women's fertility in marriage) and more detailed occupational data. Occupations for this census are designated by code numbers. For example, bargemen, watermen and lightermen are listed under occupation number 545.

Schedules of canal and inland waterway vessels can usually be found after the household schedules for the area under the heading 'List of persons not in houses'.

Boat families with a permanent house on land (and they greatly out-numbered owner-boatmen) should be in the ordinary household schedules. Boatmen tended to congregate together. For example, in the Midlands in the 1870s, it was reported there were large numbers of boatmen living at Worcester, Gloucester, Braunston and Stockton, Cowroast (near Tring), Emscote and Droitwich. A census search for one boat family may reveal details of another boat family living next door.

However, if the family left their home for part of the year to work on the canals, then they won't be in the household schedules. Or, if the wife and children are there, but some male members of the household are missing (father and son, say), they may have been away working the boat. Sometimes children were left with their grandparents while both parents worked the boat, or if there were too many children to live comfortably on board.

There was said to be a great deal of intermarriage among boat families. One reason why they preferred to marry within their community was that they were often looked down on by the non-boating population. It was also difficult for people who were not accustomed to the boating way of life to move onto the waterways.

If the family did not have a house on land then look for the census schedules for canal boats mentioned previously. 'Addresses' for canal boats, especially in the earlier censuses, seem to have given enumerators some headaches: often 'canal side' is the only address given for a boatman or canal labourer. A boatman's address could be 'canal boat' or just 'in boat on canal'. You may see boats listed as 'canal boat no. 1' then 'no. 2', 'no. 3' and so on. These are not fleet listings, just the enumerator being methodical as he worked his way along the canal bank.

The address for a boatman or boat builder might be 'the wharf' or 'canal wharf'. An enumerator in the Church Lawton area listed some 'boatsmen' in some 'out-buildings' and one in the 'open air'.

Boat names are not necessarily listed in the census schedules, although the type of boat might be included, e.g. packet boat. You may be lucky enough to find a wealth of detail; the names and fleet numbers are listed for some canal boats tied up at Blisworth Wharf on census night in 1871.

Occasionally the canal company's name or the name of the canal where the family were working is mentioned in the schedule. The Hardman family, headed by widow Fletca (*sic*) and her son and four daughters, are listed in the 1861 census as living in a canal boat and working on the Lancaster & Kendal Canal at Borwick.

Possible Problems

Father and son, and mother and daughter, would use the same first name from one generation to the next, which can cause great confusion for researchers. If a family lost a child through illness or accident, their next baby of the same sex was often named after the dead child to 'replace' him or her.

The census enumerators sometimes made mistakes when copying down a name or age. The spelling of names was not always standardized, either, and an ancestor may appear in successive censuses with his name spelt slightly differently, so try using variants of the name if conducting online searches.

Census returns can be extremely difficult to read if in poor condition, and entries can be smudged or illegible, which means there may be copying errors on census databases. Transcripts of census schedules may have been made by volunteers unfamiliar with canal occupations, so it is recommended you use 'wildcard' searches (substituting a * for a letter in a name or occupation) if you initially draw a blank when looking online for an ancestor. For example, you may see 'boat steerer' transcribed as 'boat sturer' or even 'boat stoner'.

To save time when completing the schedules, the enumerator might shorten a canal's name. For example, the Bridgwater and Taunton Canal is sometimes abbreviated to 'B and T Canal' which could make it difficult to find this 'address' using online searches.

If a boatman and his family cannot be found in their boat or house on land on census night, it is highly likely they are somewhere else on the canal network. If a family was working two boats, then relatives may appear in different parts of the canal system.

The boatman and his family or crew often stayed at canal-side inns or in lodgings because canal companies did not allow boatmen to sleep overnight at canal wharves, or permit them to have a fire in the cabin while tied up there. If they did not want to pay for lodgings, they stayed with a friend or family member.

One possibility why a boatman is 'missing' may be that he found work away from the canals. Another potential reason for difficulty in finding an ancestor is civil disobedience. People were not always keen to tell all their personal business to a government official.

There are several instances of canal boats listed in the census where the names of the inhabitants are 'not known', which suggests the enumerator was perhaps given short shrift by the boatmen when trying to obtain information. One census return notes the inhabitants of a boat in 1871 who refused to answer any questions from the enumerator.

Enumerators were only human, too. They sometimes made errors noting down families' information. Or maybe an enumerator faced with a long walk along a canal towpath to ask questions of boatmen of uncertain temper took the easy option and did not bother.

The boaters needed to make an early start so they could earn a living. George Smith of Coalville reckoned the boats would be 'in many instances twenty miles away from the officers who gave out the form' the next day when the schedules were due to be returned. There is some supporting evidence for this statement. A census schedule for a boat at Port Vale Wharf at Burslem in 1871 has the number of people on board recorded and their ages, but no names, because the boat 'went off early'.

Illiteracy may have played a part in creating gaps in the census. Smith claimed boatmen would simply throw the census schedules straight 'into the cut' because they could not read and write. Some enumerators noted that no schedule was returned to them by a particular boat, so they asked another family nearby for information. Clearly information gleaned in this way could be inaccurate.

If you still have problems finding an ancestor, they could be in hospital because they were sick or injured on census night, and may be listed in a hospital's census record.

Yet another possibility is that your ancestor may have become a pauper. Unemployed boatmen or women, the old and infirm, or owner-boatmen who had fallen on hard times, had to seek parish relief. The former occupations of pauper inmates are listed in the census records for workhouses; the Gloucester Union workhouse had several canal boatmen living there in 1861.

To protect individuals' privacy, census records are only available for the decades up to and including 1911. Many census records are online now, although like birth, marriage and death certificates you may have to pay to view them. If you do not have Internet access, county archives have copies of the census (except 1911) on microfilm or microfiche. Depending on the size of your town, your local library may have sets of census records you can consult.

Some local libraries give their members free access to Ancestry.co.uk (in the library, not for home access). Census returns are also available at the Church of Jesus Christ of Latter-Day Saints' Family History Centres (which also have some will indexes for the period up to 1858).

The census enumerators writing down the occupations of canal workers were not necessarily familiar with the industry and did not always use the correct terminology.

Case Study

When Ian Wilkes researched his family tree he traced boatmen in his family dating back to the 1770s. The canal link appears to begin with Ian's 4x great-grandfather Jeremiah Wilkes (1776–1860) listed in the 1841 census as a boatman at Alvechurch Village (no house or street number given). Ian used the census to calculate the year when Jeremiah was born. Jeremiah's son William Wilkes (1804–1862) was also a boatman, and appears in the same census with his wife Hannah and four children in Alvechurch.

In the 1851 census William is recorded at London Street, Alvechurch with his family (now with five children). His father Jeremiah had moved in with the family. Jeremiah, now in his seventies, was no longer on the canals and had found work as an agricultural labourer.

Ten years later, Jeremiah had died, and the family were living at Hopwood (Alvechurch) but his 16-year-old grandson Jeremiah was now a boatman like his father and brother, another William (1839–1923).

Their neighbours, the Witheys, were another canal-boat family and in 1865 William (Ian's 2x great-grandfather) wed the girl next door, Sarah Ann Withey.

The couple were married at Birmingham, but in 1871 the couple were still living at Hopwood. William was working as a boat labourer. A decade later, the family had moved to 55 New Road, Tipton and had two children, but William had left the canals and was working as a railway porter.

His wife Sarah's father John Withey (1814–1880) and grandfather James Withey (1782–1858) are both listed as a 'waterman' in the 1841 census. They lived at Worcester: John lived at Lowesmoor Terrace with his family, and James at Spring Street. Some of Sarah's brothers stayed on the canal network.

You may see a boater listed as a 'barge boatman' on the census return, with the 'barge' inserted next to or written over 'boatman'. If the entry refers to a narrow boatman, it may be an addition by the census enumerator.

Boatwomen's occupations may be listed as 'canal boatman' whether she assisted her husband or worked a boat on her own. Boatwomen were sometimes listed as an 'assistant' on the boat. If the family had a house or land, her occupation might be 'housekeeper'.

Census entries for land workers can sometimes be confusing, too. A family of 'boat haulers' are recorded in the 1841 census for Lancashire. George Scott, his wife Jane and seven children lived at Walton Summit (Walton-le-Dale, Preston) on the Lancaster Canal. The occupations of their teenage children James (15) and Mary (13) are listed as 'boat hauler on canal' (HO 107/0504/15-F13). One might perhaps assume the Scott family were bow-hauliers like those employed to 'haul' boats by hand on some waterways such as the Weaver Navigation.

However, on the Lancaster Canal there was a tramroad from Walton Summit to Preston; it crossed the River Ribble and joined the north and south sections of the canal (the canal company could not afford the vast expense a canal link would have entailed). Goods were trans-shipped between the north and south ends of the Lancaster canal by horse-drawn waggons along the tramroad. (The tramroad was originally an inclined plane with stationary engines providing motive power for haulage). The waggon drivers on the tramroad were known locally as 'halers' (haulers). They were employed by traders to drive the teams of horses, so it's probable the Scott family worked on the tramroad as 'boat halers'.

Some Canal Occupations Listed in the Censuses

Assistant, assistant boat gauger, barge boatman, bargeman, boat builder, boat gauger, boat maker, boat manufacturer, boat dealer, boatman, boater, boat's man, boat boy, boat hauler, boat servant, boat steerer, canal agent, canal-bank inspector, canal-bank ranger, canal-bank walker, canal-boat driver, canal boatman, canal-boat inspector, canal-boat labourer, canal-boat manager, canal foreman, canal ganger, canal labourer, canal-lock tender, canal-works engineer, captain, carpenter, carrier, clerk, engineer, flatman, keel maker, keel man, lock keeper, master, mate, mechanic, mistress of canal boat, navigator, navvy, pleasure boatman, skipper, steerer, toll clerk, toll collector, tugman, waterman, wharfinger, etc.

Please note that although people on the land often referred to all canal boats indiscriminately as 'barges', narrow boatmen did not (and still do not) like this term applied to their boats. It is also an extremely bad idea to call narrow boatmen 'bargees'. This may inadvertently cause real offence, and you may find yourself in hot water!

Several in-depth guides to the censuses have been published, including Edward Higgs's *Making sense of the census revisited: census records for England and Wales, 1801–1901: A handbook for historical researchers* (London, 2005), and P. Christian and D. Annal's *Census: The Expert Guide* (The National Archives, 2008).

Census returns and other records for Scotland can be searched and viewed online at the ScotlandsPeople website.

Ian Maxwell's books *Tracing Your Scottish Ancestors* (Pen & Sword, 2009) and *Your Irish Ancestors* (Pen & Sword, 2008) are helpful guides to Scottish and Irish family history sources.

There is a tragic lack of census data and other records for nineteenth-century Ireland. Census records from 1861–1891 were destroyed by government order during the First World War. Earlier censuses, some probate records and some Church of Ireland parish registers were destroyed in a disastrous fire at the Public Records Office at Dublin in 1922.

The 1901 and 1911 censuses for Ireland can be searched for free (by occupation as well as name) at www.census.nationalarchives.ie/.

On the same website you can view images of the household returns, the shipping returns for vessels on Ireland's inland navigations and enumerator's abstracts from the schedules.

Other Sources

Books, Newspapers and Magazines

Books on Canals
For further information on canal boatmen and their social history, Harry Hanson's *Canal People* (David & Charles, 1978) and *The Canal Boat-Men 1760–1914* (Manchester University Press, 1975) are extremely detailed with useful bibliographies and references, although the locations given for archival material are now rather out of date.

Wendy Freer's informative thesis 'Canal Boat People 1840–1970' (1991) can be downloaded from the University of Nottingham website (http://etheses.nottingham.ac.uk/). Freer's *Women and Children of the Cut* (Railway and Canal Historical Society, 1995) looks at living conditions on the canals for women and children, with special reference to narrow-boat families.

Your family may not be mentioned in a history book, but there's always a possibility that photographs or illustrations may show your ancestor's boat or the area where they worked, and at the very least will help bring their story to life.

The 'Bible' for the inland waterways is *Bradshaw's Canals and Navigable Rivers of England and Wales* by Henry de Salis. It was first published in 1904 with further editions in 1918 and 1928 (modern reprints are available). De Salis travelled every inch of the waterways network over an eleven-year period. This invaluable guide has information on canal routes, cargoes, companies, boats and much more.

If you wish to research the growth of the canal network, the most comprehensive coverage of the country (region by region) is the *Canals of the British Isles* series by Charles Hadfield, Gordon Biddle and other authors. The series, originally published by David & Charles, is now out of print. Joseph Boughey and Charles Hadfield's *British Canals: The Standard History* (Tempus Publishing, 2008) also tells the story of the inland waterways and brings it up to date.

The standard county histories (such as the Victoria series on British History Online at www.british-history.ac.uk) detail transport history and give information on evangelical missions such as those for boatmen. Your local library should have copies of county histories if you do not have Internet access.

Autobiographies often mention boats and their masters or owners, and you may spot a reminiscence of one of your ancestors. Many accounts of canal life have been published, including Sheila Stewart's *Ramlin Rose: The Boatwoman's Story* (Oxford Paperbacks, 1994), Emma Smith's *Maidens' Trip* (Bloomsbury Publishing, 2009) and Tim Wilkinson's *Hold On a Minute* (M. & M. Baldwin, 2001). Euan Corrie's *Tales from the Old Inland Waterways* (David & Charles, 2005) has vivid accounts of canal workers' lives.

Newspapers

Newspapers are useful sources for canal companies and major canal schemes. The papers reported new canal proposals and objections to the schemes, debates in Parliament regarding the construction of canals, and unusual occurrences on the waterways network. Advertisements in the newspaper's classified section will feature canal shares or canal carrying companies. Obituaries often include a 'potted biography' of the person covered. Reports of inquests on canal deaths may have individual boatmen's names.

The main town-centre libraries or alternatively your local record office should have copies of old newspapers on microfiche. Your library service may subscribe to online resources such as the *Oxford Dictionary of National Biography* and the Times Digital Library.

THE TIMES DIGITAL LIBRARY

The Library has copies of newspapers from 1785 to 1985 which you can search by date and/or key words. Although the *The Times* concentrated on London news, it included regular news updates from the provinces, and particularly juicy trials or unusual happenings were often featured.

THE BRITISH LIBRARY'S NEWSPAPER LIBRARY

This online library with searchable catalogue has British national and regional newspapers from 1800 to 1900. You can read articles from the *Penny Illustrated Paper* and the *Graphic* for free, or pay a flat fee for a 'day pass' to view up to 100 articles from other titles. Access at http://newspapers.bl.uk/blcs/.

THE *GUARDIAN* AND *OBSERVER* DIGITAL ARCHIVE

This online source has copies of issues of the *Guardian* from 1791 to 2000. You can search the archive for free, but if you want to read or print off an article in full, you must purchase a 'day pass' which allows you to download as many articles as you wish for twenty-four hours. Access at http:/archive.guardian.co.uk.

Trade and Maritime Directories

Among the most useful late Georgian and Victorian trade directories are those by Edward Baines (1820s), Pigot (1820s onwards), William White (1830s) and Kelly; the Kelly directories continued in print into the

Case Study

Charles Baxton (or Bexson), steerer of the *Tilbury*, his 'hand' William Taylor and an unidentified 18-year-old lad were killed on the Regent's Canal on Friday 3 October 1874. A steam tug, the *Ready*, was towing five 'monkey boats' (narrow boats). The *Jane* was attached to the *Ready*, with the *Dee* and the *Tilbury* (as a pair) behind it, and the *Limehouse* and the *Hawksbury* following, also paired together.

Suddenly the *Tilbury*, which was carrying several tons of gunpowder and benzoline (fuel), went up in a massive explosion which caused widespread destruction. The incredibly loud bang was heard miles away. The North Gate bridge (also known as Macclesfield bridge) over the canal was demolished, and many houses and windows damaged. The *Tilbury* was destroyed and the *Limehouse*, which was right behind it, sank. Luckily, the crew of the *Limehouse* struggled to shore. The other boats and their crews survived.

During the coroner's inquest, which began at Marylebone workhouse on 3 October, several details of the deceased boatmen, who worked for the Grand Junction Canal Co., were published in the newspapers. Baxton, a 35-year-old Loughborough man, left a wife and 'three or four' children behind. Taylor (26) was from Brierley Hill, and his parents worked for Price & Co.

The dead anonymous teenager was photographed before his funeral so he could be identified. His father, 'a feeble old man' who lived at Oldbury, later identified him as Jonathan Holloway. He said his son had left home twelve months earlier (perhaps to work on the boats).

Several boatmen gave evidence to the inquest, including Edward Hall, a Braunston boatman who was steering the *Limehouse*. He identified Taylor's body. William White (a 'labourer' on the *Dee*) and Francis Clark, a Birmingham boatman who was steering the *Ready*, also testified. Clark saw a blue flame on the *Tilbury* just before the explosion.

Other canal workers were also called as witnesses, including porter John Scott and John Walker, an invoice clerk, both employees at the Grand Junction Canal wharf.

The jury gave their verdict after many days of listening to witnesses and scientific evidence. They believed a fire or the oil lamp in the boatmen's cabin caused vapour from the benzoline to ignite, causing the explosion. The captain of the *Dee*, John Edwards, admitted they had a fire in their cabin so they could boil a kettle.

The jury found the Grand Junction Canal Co. guilty of gross negligence, because although their boats regularly carried hazardous cargoes such as benzoline, gunpowder and petroleum, boatmen were not given any instructions on how to carry dangerous substances safely. It was reported that the boatmen often smoked and lit candles in their cabins. (*The Times*, 5, 8, 12, 13 and 20 October 1874.)

The names of individuals mentioned in newspaper reports should be treated with a certain amount of caution; the reporter's spelling may be inaccurate. The author was unable to locate a Charles Baxton or Bexson of the right age in Loughborough in the 1871 census (three years before the disaster). However, a 'boatman', Charles Bexon, is listed living in a house on Canal Bank, Loughborough in 1871. Bexon's age is given as 39; he was born at Loughborough. Bexon had a wife, Sarah (39), and two children: Thomas J. (7) and Eliza S. (2). Man and wife were both born at Loughborough.

If this is the same man killed in the Regent's Canal tragedy, it is possible one or more children had been born since the 1871 census. However, when one searches the 1881 census (using, for example, www.TheGenealogist.co.uk or other online census services) a Sarah Bexon (47) is listed as the head of the family, but she has moved to 33 King Street, Loughborough along with her children Thomas (18) and Eliza (11). No other children are mentioned.

Charles Bexon has seemingly disappeared from the census, which may mean he was the unfortunate boatman who lost his life.

One of the other boatmen who died, Jonathan Holloway, is listed along with his father and mother Sarah in the 1871 census as living at 176 West Bromwich Street, Oldbury. Father and son's occupations are given as 'labourer in an iron works'.

Memories of this tragedy lingered for a long time on the waterways. The canal bridge, which was rebuilt, was known as 'Blow-up Bridge' ever after by boatmen.

twentieth century. Local guidebooks and directories should be used with caution because they weren't necessarily up to date when printed. To save costs, the same printing plates were sometimes re-used for several years afterwards.

Most local record offices have trade and street directories spanning many decades. Some archives have now put digital images of trade and street directories on their websites as an aid for family history researchers.

The University of Leicester has a searchable digital library of directories from the 1760s onwards. The library includes directories by Pigot, Kelly and the Post Office; you can search by location or by decade at www.historicaldirectories.org/hd/index.asp.

The London Guildhall Library has a fine collection of trade directories at www.cityoflondon.gov.uk/Corporation/LGNL_Services/Leisure_and_cult ure/Libraries/City_of_London_libraries/guildhall_lib.htm.

Google Books has a selection of topographical and trade directories such as Gore's *Liverpool Directory* (1766), those by Baines and White and some maritime directories such as Marwood's at http://books.google.com/.

Parliamentary Papers

Parliamentary papers are often overlooked as a resource by family historians. During the nineteenth century Parliament commissioned many special reports into conditions in industry. A huge amount of evidence was gathered on coal, cotton, iron and steel, and other trades. The Royal Commission reports form part of the vast numbers of 'Sessional' papers printed for every parliamentary session.

The most interesting for genealogists are probably the Command Papers, published 'by command' of the reigning monarch. Command Papers are often called 'Blue Books' because they originally had blue covers. Digital images of parliamentary papers such as Select Committee reports can be accessed in the reading rooms of TNA.

Command Papers with information on living conditions for boatmen and their families include the *Report of the Select Committee on Sunday Trading* (1841) and the *Report of the Select Committee on the Canal Boats Act (1877) Amendment Bill* (1884) which contain eyewitness reports of canal life. The *Royal Commission on Canals and Waterways* (1906) was an exhaustive study of the canal network.

Catalogues and indexes are available to help you explore Blue Books at TNA, the British Library, large reference libraries and the Parliamentary

Archives. You may also find these books (now out of print) helpful: Maurice F. Bond's *Guide to the Records of Parliament* (HMSO, 1971), W.R. Powell's *Local History from Blue Books* (Historical Association, 1962) and *Sources for English Local History* (Phillimore, 1994).

The Parliamentary Archives

Visitors to the Parliamentary Archives can view Command Papers for free in the search room. The archives hold unpublished petitions for and against proposed canals and railways, and minutes of evidence from Select Committees relating to the transport network.

Online Resources for Parliamentary Papers

Most digitized parliamentary papers are subscriber only (and prohibitively expensive). There is information on parliamentary papers on the Parliamentary Archives website. You can download a free guide to family history at http://www.parliament.uk/business/publications/parliamentary-archives/archives-highlights/archives-family-history/.

Guide to publications and records at www.parliament.uk/business/publications.

Aston mill, Stone, Trent & Mersey Canal. Postcard, c.1903.

Guide to parliamentary papers which are available at www. parliament.uk/business/publications/parliamentary-archives/archives-electronic/parliamentary-papers.

Online Parliamentary Archives Catalogue Portcullis at www. parliament.uk/business/publications/parliamentary-archives/archives-catalogue.

Parliamentary Archives, Houses of Parliament, London, SW1A 0PW, United Kingdom; email: archives@parliament.uk; tel: 0207 219 3074.

Proquest/Chadwyck Healey: the House of Commons parliamentary papers for 1801 to 2004 have been digitized by Proquest/Chadwyck Healey. This online digital collection is only available through university and academic libraries but you can access it for free at the reading rooms at TNA at http://parlipapers.chadwyck.co.uk/marketing/index.jsp.

British History Online: read a selection of House of Commons and House of Lords journals for free at the British History Online website at www.british-history.ac.uk.

Historic Hansard: parliamentary debates from 1803 to 2005 at http:// hansard.millbanksystems.com/.

The Victorian Times Project: a small number of parliamentary papers concerning the Canal Boats Acts and some archive images at http:// victoria.cdlr.strath.ac.uk/index.php.

Google Books: a limited number of parliamentary papers online at http://books.google.com/.

A2

HEALTH (CANAL BOAT) REGISTERS

If you know the name of the boat that your ancestor worked on or owned, or the waterway where they worked, then you can use this information to search the canal-boat health registers and gauging tables (registers) mentioned earlier.

How To Find Health (Canal Boat) Registers

Local record offices and some large libraries are the best place to look for sanitary inspection registers, boat certificates and canal-boat inspectors' notebooks and journals and reports under the Canal Boats Acts of 1877, 1884 and the Public Health Act of 1934. The health registers that have survived are catalogued under a variety of different names in various archives. (Some are listed under the appropriate county archive in Section B below.)

In some archives the registers are easy to find because they are clearly catalogued as 'registers of canal boats and barges'. Other archives have catalogued the registers by reference to the waterway where the boats worked. Some archives have not catalogued health registers separately and (especially if searching online) you may have to try several different searches to hunt them down. If an archive does not have an online catalogue, search some of their holdings via the A2A search engine.

Public-health records in county archives are the likeliest place to find the registers and related sanitary records: Medical Officer of Health reports, sanitary inspector reports, inspector of nuisances, etc. For example, Cheshire Record Office holds health registers created by several sanitary authorities: Chester City, Northwich, Nantwich and Runcorn Urban District Councils.

Health registers may also be kept with port records. For example, the Port of London Sanitary Authority was responsible for checking canal boats in its area complied with the Canal Boats Acts. At Bristol, sanitary reports on canal boats from 1885 were made by the Port of Bristol Medical Officer of Health and are catalogued under that series (33416).

Try online searches in record-office catalogues or on A2A for 'canal-boat register', 'boat register', 'health register', 'Canal Boat(s) Act', '(canal) boat inspector', 'sanitary inspector', 'health inspector', 'medical officer of health', 'sanitary authority', 'inspector's journal', 'breaches of the Canal Boat(s) Act' or 'complaints under the Canal Boat(s) Act'. Remember to limit your search by date from 1877 onwards (the date of the first Canal Boats Act).

Repositories do not necessarily have examples of each type of record, and some health registers are no longer kept at their original local authority. Not all local authorities complied with the Canal Boats Acts so a health register may never have existed for your area of interest. Some registers like the one for Goole were accidentally destroyed. On a few occasions mistakes were made when compiling a register, such as two boats being registered with identical numbers by the same authority.

Canal boats were often registered near where they were built, but not necessarily registered in the place where they usually worked, so you may need to broaden your search to other counties. For example, the Northwich canal-boat inspector's pocket book records an inspection of narrow boat *Beaver*, No. 357, registered at Daventry. The *Beaver* was owned by Henry Seddon & Co., a well-known salt manufacturer and canal carrier. His fleet of boats were regulars on the Trent & Mersey Canal and further afield.

Owners registered their boats for the maximum number of people permitted under the Act. Readers should not fall into the trap of assuming the number of adults and children each boat was permitted to carry was the actual number of people living on board. An owner would not want the expense of re-registering the boat each time the size of the

---

Case Study – **Burland**

This boat was registered at Nantwich (No. 83) in September 1909. Its master was John Howard, and it was owned by H. Chesworth & Son Ltd, Pillory Street, Nantwich. It was licensed to carry three adults, and its usual route was through Nantwich, Wrenbury and the Potteries carrying coal, ashes, salt, bricks and pipes. A note scribbled by the inspector indicates the boat's certificate was cancelled in July 1914, perhaps because it had moved away. Three years later it was re-registered as boat No. 87 (CRO LUN 4452/1).

crew changed, perhaps because another boat lad was hired, or if the family working the boat had another baby.

The health registers, if kept accurately, can give clues to changes of ownership, master or boat name. The inspector sometimes lost track of a boat ('no trace') if it disappeared from his area. He noted if the boat had been 'cut up' or if the owner was deceased.

The quality of the information in some canal-boat inspectors' journals can be suspect: there may be some 'ghost' boats. It was not unknown for an inspector to re-copy earlier entries if he could not be bothered to visit the canal, perhaps because he was too busy. In the interim some boats might have moved to another area.

The registers are not always easy to find in the catalogues. Fortunately, archives such as Gloucestershire Record Office, some family history

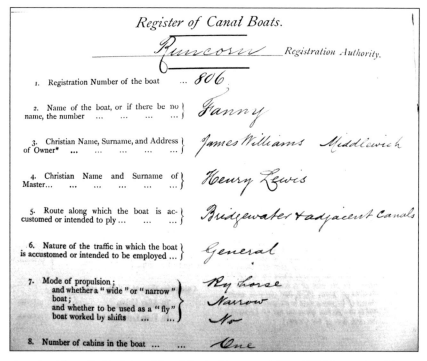

An extract from the Register of Canal Boats, Runcorn, 1883–1897. Narrow boat Fanny, *no. 806, was registered on 5 March 1884.* Fanny, *owned by James Williams of Middlewich, was permitted to travel along the Bridgewater Canal and adjacent waterways. The boat's master was Henry Lewis, and accommodation was limited to three persons in the aft cabin under the 1877 Canal Boats Act. CRO LUR/57/5.*

societies and a specialist publisher have transcribed some health registers (see Sections B2 and C). The Gloucester Docks waterways archive has databases for over twenty health registers and information on where some registers are kept.

Fleet lists for some canal carriers have been published in the specialist waterways magazines, and these often include the place where each boat was registered and its registration number.

Health registers only rarely give a boat's place of construction but they can be used to cross-reference a boat owner's details gleaned from the gauging registers or tables (Section A3). For example, if an owner-boatman regularly worked for a large canal carrier such as Fellows, Morton & Clayton, and used one of their toll permits, the gauging table showed the carrier (FMC) as the 'owner' in case a query arose over the cargo. However, the health register will reveal that the boatman actually owned the boat, not the carrier he worked for.

GAUGING TABLES (REGISTERS) AND OTHER COMPANY RECORDS

If you know the name of your ancestor's boat from the census or other source, but do not have any other details, bear in mind that boat names were often duplicated around the canal network. There were probably several boats named *Sarah*, *Lily* or *Elizabeth*, say, in the same census year.

The gauging registration number for your ancestor's boat (if known) should uniquely identify it. If you know the gauging number of the boat you can use the gauging records to ascertain more information on its owners. Sometimes gauging registers include the history of the boat's ownership and the place where built.

Each boat had a gauge record which listed its name, date registered, type of freight carried, the boat owner's name and address. The boatman's name is unlikely to be on the gauging register unless he owned the boat.

The gauge or gauging tables are archived under several names: gauge books, registers, tables or sheets. Only a few gauging tables survive from before the mid-1840s. Wooden canal boats had a finite working life and companies probably saw no point in keeping records for craft that had been broken up because of old age.

Case Study

The Grand Junction Canal gauging register for 1818 gives the name of each boat's owner and a brief address. Boat No. 2217 on the register was owned by Howard & Sons of Box Moor (Hemel Hempstead). Boat No. 2222 belonged to Joseph George of Wolverhampton (TNA RAIL 830/56).

TNA has a Grand Junction Canal Company (GJCC) gauging register for 1818 (RAIL 830/56) and a collection of BCN registers (RAIL 810/403-18). The Gloucester Docks waterways archive has a collection of nineteenth- and twentieth-century gauge books, registers and sheets, including some early nineteenth-century GJCC registers and tables for the Trent Navigation (BW98). The Ellesmere Port waterways archive has gauging tables for boats on the River Weaver (BWWN20).

Nottinghamshire Archives has Trent Navigation gauging registers (DD/NM/1) from 1856–1908. Nottinghamshire Family History Society has published an index to these tables, compiled by Brian and Robert Widdowson. See the Nottinghamshire Family History Society Record Series Vol. 104, 'Boatmen, Boat Owners and Boat Builders'.

If a photograph has survived of your ancestor's boat, you can glean information from the registration numbers painted on its side. A canal boat bore several different markings, depending on who owned it, where it was registered and the canals where it worked.

A Fellows, Morton & Clayton (FMC) boat of the early twentieth century typically displayed five numbers: its FMC fleet number, its Waterman's Hall registration number, its health registration number (see Chapter 4), a Grand Junction Canal gauging number and a BCN gauging number.

Several titles on canal art and boat markings have been published, including Edward Paget-Tomlinson's *Colours of the Cut* (Landmark Countryside Collection, 2004).

Toll Records

Toll tickets can help you track a boatman's movements and investigate vessel and company history on the waterways. Each boatman or steerer carried a toll ticket showing the type of cargo they carried and its weight. The cargo's weight was checked by the toll collector or 'gauger' (see Chapter 5).

Each toll ticket contained details of the boatman and his steerer, cargo, route and company name. These are rare items but sometimes copies were made for canal-company records. The tolls system lasted until the nationalization of the canal network in 1948.

Toll tickets can be found in local record offices and the waterways archives under a variety of names: canal permits, traffic tickets, barge check sheets, declaration notes and so on, but they all performed the

---

Case Study 1

A Shropshire Union Canal Carrying Co. toll ticket dated 16 February 1949 records a journey by Thomas Clayton of Oldbury boat the *Spey*. The boat delivered fuel oil from Stanlow to Langley Green and its steerer was J. Jinks (TWA EP D7619).

Case Study 2

'Declaration notes' contain similar details. A note dated 12 September 1949 records that Fellows, Morton & Clayton boat *Mullet* permitted the steerer J. Shaw to carry a cargo of flour between Ellesmere Port and Wolverhampton (TWA EP D1954).

---

same function. The ticket had the boat's name and number and showed the toll collector or clerk how much cargo the boat was carrying and for which firm.

Tonnage books often include captains' names, vessel name, the date, the cargo carried and customer. Daily 'passings' of boats (traffic records) at locks, tunnels or toll houses may yield the name of your ancestor's boat and its master or steerer. The log book for the Harecastle tunnel notes that the boat *Otter* steered by R. Barnett entered the tunnel at 8.10 a.m. on 15 December 1959 and emerged at 9.20 am (TWA EP D7074).

Staff Records

Use the NRA index, Virtual Waterways Archive Catalogue and A2A search engine as illustrated in Chapter 2 to find company and carrier records. Try searches for 'staff' or 'employees' plus the company name, but there may only be a limited amount of documentary material (if any) for small independent carriers. The following sources may also yield names.

Canal-company records such as minute books, journals, cash books or wage books may have payments to workers such as boatmen. For example, the Birmingham Canal Company journals for 1770–1778 (RAIL 810/242-6) include payments to boatman Job Lloyd and boatwoman Hannah Hipkiss, who began working boats after her husband died.

Case Study

In February and March 1813, engineer Thomas Fowls took on some extra hands to make repairs at the Weston Canal (a cut from Frodsham on the River Weaver to Weston Point). The wages book for the works includes the names of flatmen Thomas Bibby and James and John Holdford who transported earth and cinders to and from the site (CRO D1361/2).

Wage books, vessels' log books, account books, day wage sheets, pension records and rent records are all useful sources for workers. Wage books should list employees and the section of canal or company premises where they were employed, number of days worked and wages received, and sometimes pension payments. You may come across managers' comments on individual workers, perhaps if they gave exceptional service or misbehaved.

Pension books or friendly society records may have lists of workers and the dates when they made contributions, or received their pension, sick pay or perhaps help with the cost of a funeral.

Canal companies owned a great deal of land and properties. As mentioned in Chapter 5, land staff often had a company house, and rent books will record payments and dates of tenancy. If rent books no longer survive, then company correspondence or minute books may yield information on properties and tenants.

Case Study

Charles Wharton, a carpenter at Wheelock on the Trent & Mersey Canal for the NSR, was 21 years old when he started working for the company in 1882. He earned 4s 5d per day, and his house rent of 2s per week was 'included in his wages'. When Charles retired on 30 June 1928, he was given a present of £10 and a pension of 5s per week, supplemented by another 5s per week from a benevolent fund for the first twelve months (TWA E P 20001.146).

> **Case Study 1**
>
> The Shropshire Union Railway and Canal Co. (SURCC) staff register for 1862–1897 lists wages for permanent employees such as Thomas Postings, 'Captain of Powder Boat' at Ellesmere Port. No date of first employment is given, but Postings was on a regular wage of 40s per week. His name in the ledger is crossed out in red ink and there is an entry for the date when he died and left the company's employment: 12 February 1887.
>
> Although boatmen and steerers were usually paid by the job they may still be listed in staff registers and wage books for permanent staff. The SURCC register lists occasional payments to boatmen (no date) such as steerer Edward Nixon for 'boating pig iron' at 6½d per ton (TNA RAIL 623/67).

If your ancestor was injured or killed at work, he may appear in the company's accident register, along with any compensation paid under the Workmen's Compensation Acts. Employers were first made liable to pay compensation to workers injured in 1880, although initially workers had to prove the company was negligent. Statutory compensation was introduced by the Workmen's Compensation Acts of 1897 and 1906.

Employees who were badly hurt or on permanent sick leave may be listed in company pension books, insurance records or in Workmen's Compensation Act judgements in county court cases at your local record office. Arthur Shenton, a watchman and labourer at Etruria, drowned in the canal on 29 December 1930. The NSR ledger records a payment

> **Case Study 2**
>
> The Birmingham Canal Navigations Cottage Rent Journal (Midsummer and Lady Day) has lists of employees, locations and the dates when they paid rent. Three properties are listed at Ludgate Hill (Birmingham & Fazeley Canal) for the quarter up to Lady Day in 1912. The houses were rented by E. Humphries (3s per week), H. Jones and H. Webb (who paid 5s per week) (TNA RAIL 810/487).

(presumably to his widow or children) of £307 10s plus £7 10s court fees (TWA EPort 20001.146.)

Details of accidents to staff and compensation sometimes crop up in canal-inspectors' correspondence, too.

British Waterways Board (BWB)

The waterways archives at Gloucester Docks and Ellesmere Port both have BWB staff records. Use the Virtual Waterways Archive Catalogue and A2A to explore their collections.

The BWB Northern Region records are archived at the Wakefield office of West Yorkshire Archives Service (C299). Warwickshire County Record Office (CR1590) and Lancashire Record Office (DDX 1052) also have BWB collections.

Gloucestershire Record Office has records for BWB and its former incarnations, mostly relating to the River Severn and Gloucester and Sharpness Canal (D2460).

These records are chiefly administrative and financial; there's a list of records filed under D2460 on the Gloucestershire Record Office online catalogue.

For Scotland, many BWB records are still held privately by British Waterways Scotland (www.britishwaterways.co.uk/scotland). The main British Waterways holdings at TNAS (BW) relate to the Crinan Canal and date from 1878–1959 (BW1).

In Ireland, the Office of Public Works (OPW) had responsibility for the canal and waterways network. Its archive is kept at The National Archives of Ireland.

Apprentices

Narrow boatmen did not usually take formal apprentices. Watermen and lightermen on the Thames took apprentices and the registers of apprentice bindings are archived in the Company of Watermen and Lightermen records at London Metropolitan Archives; an index is available.

Under the Statute of Artificers (1563) no one could enter a trade or profession such as that of boat builder or carpenter unless they first served an apprenticeship. Between 1710 and 1811 stamp duty was payable when a young person was apprenticed, and the Commissioners of Stamps kept records of the payments they received. The Apprenticeship Books (IR1 at TNA) give the name of the apprentice and the name and address of his or her master.

The Statute of Artificers was repealed in 1814. Formal apprenticeships were no longer compulsory but young people apprenticed as carpenters, masons, boat builders, etc. may be listed in company staff records such as wage books.

Apprenticeship indentures (legal documents formalizing apprenticeship) may be found in family papers, parish records (where a pauper child was apprenticed into a trade) or company records. For example, the Bridgewater Estates collection (Salford Local History Library) has indentures and draft indentures for workmen such as carpenters, joiners and blacksmiths.

Friendly Societies and Trade Unions

Friendly society and trade-union records may record payments made by or to workers relating to sick pay or other expenses. The records for the Register of Friendly Societies from 1784–1999 are at TNA (series FS).

Merseyside Maritime Museum has early twentieth-century financial records for the north-west division of the Seamen's and Boatmen's Friend Society (P-CC-SB).

Nottinghamshire Archives has records for the Incorporated Seamen and Boatmen's Friend Society (DD/PL/7/113). This organization had a

Canal boat on the River Trent near Wychnor (Wichnor). The Trent & Mersey canal connected to the river close by. Staffordshire and Warwickshire Past and Present, Vol. II (*William Mackenzie, c.1880*).

magazine called the *Waterman* and Birmingham Central Library has some copies. Glasgow City Archives has some records for the Canal Boatmen's Institute and Port Dundas Mission (TD1301).

The NRA index can help locate union records. Local record offices sometimes have small collections, and the waterways archives. The Labour History Archive at the People's History Museum (Manchester) has some union records. Use the A2A search engine to explore its holdings.

The TGWU archive (which includes National Transport Federation records) is at Warwick University library (MSS 126). There's an online catalogue at www2.warwick.ac.uk/services/library/mrc/images/tgwu/.

River Navigations

A complete survey of river navigation sources is beyond the scope of this book. River navigation organizations were generally much earlier in date than canals. However, the same broad principles for research apply as for canals. For ancestors born before 1750 you will have to rely on parish registers and probate records if no company records are available. Check quarter sessions records in local record offices for the 1795 registers of

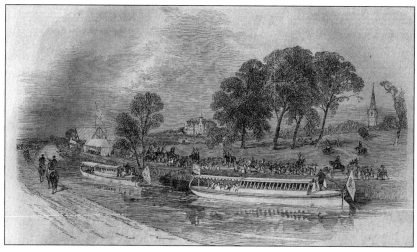

Queen Victoria's state barges on the Bridgewater Canal. The boats were specially made for her visit to north-west England in 1851. One boat was for the Queen, the other was for her retinue. The stern of each boat was decorated with the Earl of Ellesmere's coat of arms. The Queen's boat was painted white with gold mouldings, and was upholstered inside with crimson satin. Illustrated London News, *18 October 1851.*

boats and barges or 'registers of vessels'. Use the online NRA indexes, Virtual Waterways Archive Catalogue and A2A to locate company records.

Merseyside Record Office holds the Upper Mersey Navigation Commissioners' records. The John Goodchild collection at Wakefield holds papers for river navigations including the Aire & Calder.

Gloucestershire Archives has collections relating to the River Severn and the Trent Navigation Co. Nottingham University Library also has a Trent Navigation Co. collection. Berkshire Record Office has a major Thames Conservancy collection. The Ellesmere Port waterways archive has an extensive archive relating to the River Weaver Navigation, and a family history help sheet. Cheshire Record Office has an important collection of River Weaver papers.

B
ARCHIVES AND REPOSITORIES

The most important collections of canal records are kept at the national archives for each country, local record offices and the waterways archives. The records you need may not be concentrated in one area. If time and resources permit, it's a good idea to explore the catalogues in the record offices for the counties through which your ancestor's canal passed.

Sections B1, B2 and B3 contain a broad selection of archives, libraries and repositories with canal-related materials; there are many more. Websites and contact details are subject to change, so the golden rule is to check each archive's location and opening times before travelling. Original documents may be stored off-site so you may need to give the archivist advance notice (sometimes up to two weeks) if you wish to view a particular item. The vast majority of the archives listed have photographic collections so these are not always mentioned in each listing.

THE NATIONAL ARCHIVES (TNA)

TNA holds the bulk of the surviving canal-company records: minute books, wage books, correspondence, deeds of partnership, bankruptcy orders, canal share certificates and shareholders' registers, prospectuses, pamphlets, accounts, maps, deposited plans, photographs and surveys, etc. Canal records are archived with docks, road and railway records in addition to many other records. TNA Research Guide 'Domestic Records Information 83 (Canals)' gives an overview of the many types of record available.

Board of Trade Records

During the 1850s the Board of Trade (BT) had overall responsibility for the canal network. The most important BT records for canals are in general correspondence: BT 22. Establishment Department (responsible for staff, pay and other services) papers are in BT 13. Finance Department papers including accounts and pensions: BT 15. Companies Department correspondence and papers: BT 58. BT papers on the regulation of goods' transportation rates and fares (Railway and Canal Traffic Acts 1854–1894) are in RAIL 1038.

By law, every canal company had to submit a return once a year to the Companies Registration Office under the Railway and Canal Traffic Act of 1888. Each return included the company's name, the canal the company was associated with and the address of the company's main office. The records for 1889–1944 (eighty-four volumes) are kept at TNA under the BT 283 series. There is an alphabetical finding aid for canal companies (BT 283/84). This section of the Railway and Canal Traffic Act was not repealed until 1962.

Ministry of Transport Records

The Ministry of Transport (series MT) took over the functions and records of the Board of Trade Railway Department in 1919. Class MT also includes the records of the Railway and Canal Division (founded in 1873) and Railway Rates Tribunal (1921–1949): see MT 56, MT 68 and MT 77, and J 75, HO 45 and more.

During the First World War the canal network was supervised by the Canal Control Committee (1917–1920): see MT 52, MT 49 and T 186.

After several departmental changes, the Docks and Canal Division (1934–1962) supervised the canal network. Correspondence and papers are in MT 52, MT 115 and MT 140. MT 52 includes Canal Defence Advisory Committee (1939–1942) and Central Canal Committee (1942) papers. Defence planning records are in MT 6, MT 47, MT 50 and MT 63 (which includes labour and working conditions), with canal records for the London region in MT 64-5, MT 70 .

The canal network was nationalized on 1 January 1948 under the Transport Act of the previous year. The Ministry of Transport remained as supervisory body, but day-to-day running of the canals was transferred to the British Transport Commission (BTC), which set up the new Docks and Inland Waterways Executive.

The Transport Act of 1962 reorganized the Ministry of Transport and National Transport Division B took over the canal network. Its correspondence and papers from 1939–1982 can be found in MT 88 (including the Bowes Committee of Inquiry into Canals and Inland Waterways during 1956–1958) and MT 124. MT 89 has papers for International Transport Division B.

British Transport Historical Records (BTHR)
The BTC records (including those from earlier administrative bodies) later became part of the BTHR collection. British Waterways Board records and Inland Waterways Executive (class AN) papers also became part of the BTHR archive.

The BWB and BTC papers, including the Docks and Inland Waterways Executive records, are in series AN 71 and AN 76-9.

The British Transport Historical Records (BTHR) collection is the most fruitful source for canal history. The chief finding aid is the BTHR card index in the document reading room. A booklet with notes on how to use the finding aids is available. There are some additional finding aids in the research enquiries room.

The BTHR archive has almost 150 records series and only a brief overview can be given here.

The RAIL class has papers for private canal companies which were nationalized, including those swallowed up by railways. The main series of records relating to individual canal companies, including those nationalized in 1947, are in RAIL 800-899.

Companies changed name over time, and a search of the TNA catalogue often elicits several sets of records for each firm, particularly when they had dealings with other companies.

You may find TNA's 'Domestic Records Information Guide 82' helpful in relation to railway staff records, although you will need the name of the railway company that owned the waterway your ancestor worked on (see Chapter 5).

- Aire & Calder Navigation RAIL 800. A list of its boats on the Leeds and Liverpool Canal (early 1800s) is in RAIL 800/250.
- Birmingham and Liverpool Junction Canal Co: RAIL 808.
- Birmingham Canal Navigation Co. (BCN) minutes and reports from 1767–1948: RAIL 810. BCN company minutes, share registers, rent rolls, tonnage registers and more. BCN journals from 1770–1934: RAIL 810/242-287. Traffic registers ('up and down boats at various locks'): RAIL 810/394-6 and gauge registers from 1873–1945: RAIL 810/403-418. RAIL 1007/504 has BCN records when owned by the London and Midland Scottish Railway.
- Chester Canal Navigation Co.: RAIL 816.
- Dudley Canal Navigation Co.: RAIL 824.
- Ellesmere Canal Co.: RAIL 827.
- Ellesmere and Chester Canal Co.: RAIL 826.
- Erewash Canal Co.: RAIL 828.
- Grand Junction Canal Company minute books, stock and share registers, boat registers, cash books, account books, invoice books and staff records from 1793–1928: RAIL 830 and PRO 30/26. Company minutes are under RAIL 830/5, and the gauging register for 1818 is in RAIL 830/56.
- Grand Union Canal Company (GUCC) minute books: RAIL 831-2. The GUCC index: RAIL 860/87.
- Lancaster Canal Navigation Co.: RAIL 844.
- Leeds and Liverpool Canal Co.: RAIL 846.
- Liskeard and Looe Union Canal Co.: RAIL 367.
- Monmouthshire Railway and Canal Co.: RAIL 500.
- Montgomeryshire Canal Co.: RAIL 852.
- Oxford Canal Co.: RAIL 855.
- Regent's Canal Co.: RAIL 860.
- River Weaver Navigation records from 1721–1948 include tonnage books and registers of flats and boats with captains' names: RAIL 883.

- Shropshire Union Railway and Canal Co.: RAIL 618-9 and RAIL 623 which includes company minutes (RAIL 623/19), tolls (RAIL 623/64), rent registers (RAIL 623/60-1) and staff books for 1844–1897 (RAIL 623/66-7.) RAIL 623/68 is an index to the staff register.
- Staffordshire and Worcester Canal Navigation Co.: RAIL 871.
- St Helens Canal (Sankey Brook Navigation): RAIL 1007/580.
- Trent & Mersey Canal Co. company minutes, stocks and share registers: RAIL 878.
- Trent Navigation Co. company minutes, reports, accounts for 1782–1948: RAIL 879.
- Warwick and Birmingham Canal Navigation: RAIL 881.
- Worcester and Birmingham Canal Co.: RAIL 886.
- Wyrley and Essington Canal Co.: RAIL 887.

Canal Board and Harbour Undertakings papers are in RAIL 1112. Reports and accounts of various railway and canal companies are under RAIL 1116-7. Subscription contracts for canals such as the Birmingham Canal Navigations and Coventry Canal are in RAIL 1162 and RAIL 1163. Pickford's Ltd records including minutes and shares records are in RAIL 1133.

Special collections include the RAIL 1019 and RAIL 1029 series: maps, plans, reports and surveys for canals and inland waterways.

The BTHR archive also includes publications such as books and pamphlets on canals and waterways (ZLIB) and periodicals (ZPER) from 1675–1982, some of which were published by the canal companies.

Other holdings at TNA
TNA holds some records for Scotland's inland waterways: the Caledonian, Crinan, Forth and Clyde and Union Canals. The Treasury papers include public works in Scotland such as the Caledonian and Crinan Canals: T 1. Caledonian Canal accounts and papers are in T82 and maintenance records in T161.

Legal papers such as winding up orders for canal companies can be found in J 13. See also J 14, J 45, J 100 and J 107 for other legal records. Bankruptcy papers for canal companies can be found in BT 226 and in the Bankruptcy Courts and Commissioners series (B).

Statistics for collective wage agreements for manual workers (including transport and communications) for 1853–1982 can be found under LAB 83.

Health and Education

Information on local sanitary conditions may be found in local Government Board papers (class MH 12.)

The Chief Inspector of Canal Boats John Brydone's correspondence for 1883–1889 is in MH 32/94.

Some Ministry of Health and Local Government files relating to canals are in HLG 52. Education department (ED) files have information on canal-boat children's schooling from the 1870s to the 1940s, including summaries of returns: ED 14/ED 10-12.

A report on the Brentford school for canal-boat children is in ED 11/91.

HMI Mr H.J.R. Murray's papers as representative of Board of Education on the Committee on Living-in on Canal Boats (1920) and other information on canal-boat children: ED 11/93. London school-board rulings regarding canal-boat children: ED 14/18. The Committee of the Privy Council on Education minutes and reports are in ED 17, including the minutes for 1895–1896 which mention canal children: ED 17/66.

More Ministry of Education records concerning canals for 1945–1955 are in ED 147/15-16, and records for 1956–1963 are in ED 147/517.

When visiting TNA you need a reader's ticket to view original documents; take two forms of identification with you (details on the website). A reader's ticket is not necessary to view copies of documents on microfilm or microfiche such as census records.

The National Archives, Kew, Richmond, Surrey, TW9 4DU; www.nationalarchives.gov.uk; email contact form: www.nationalarchives. gov.uk/contact/form; tel: 0208 876 3444. Search TNA catalogue at www. nationalarchives.gov.uk/catalogue/default.asp.

Domestic Records Information Guide 82 (Railways):
www.nationalarchives.gov.uk/records/research-guides/railway-staff.htm.

Domestic Records Information 83 (Canals):
www.nationalarchives.gov.uk/records/research-guides/canals.htm.

Domestic Records Information 92 (Merchant Shipping Crew Lists):
www.nationalarchives.gov.uk/records/research-guides/merchant-shipping-crewlists-agreements-1747-1860.htm.

Domestic Records Information 94 (Merchant Shipping Registration): www.nationalarchives.gov.uk/records/research-guides/merchant-shipping-registration-1786-1994.htm.

TNA DocumentsOnline

Download copies of wills proved in the Prerogative Court of Chancery (PCC) from 1384–1858, some death-duty registers from 1796–1811 and other records (a fee is payable).

Copies of a select number of nineteenth-century Poor Law union and workhouse records (MH 12) can be downloaded free of charge. www.nationalarchives.gov.uk/documentsonline.

LOCAL RECORD OFFICES IN ENGLAND AND WALES

Your record office or county archive should be your first port of call for census returns, parish records, bishops' transcripts, Poor Law settlement papers, electoral registers, probate records, school records, historic photographs, diaries and so on.

Quarter sessions records in local record offices will include deposited maps, plans and deeds for canals, registers of vessels and applications to register vessels (under the 1795 Act) with the Clerk of the Peace (see Section E).

If your ancestor came into contact with the law at some point, perhaps because he or she suffered an accident, or was involved in a misdemeanour, they may be mentioned in quarter sessions, magistrates' courts (petty sessions) or coroners' records (inquests) at your local record office.

For example, quarter sessions records at Staffordshire Record Office include a number of convictions of boatmen under the Canal Acts: wasting water from locks, allowing a boat to hit lock gates and so on. Depositions (witness statements) may have names of canal workers or boatmen if they were accused of theft, for instance.

Poor Law settlement certificates helped establish a person's entitlement to relief from their home parish. The certificates enabled men or women to seek work in other parishes without the fear of being sent back home post-haste.

Poor Law officials expended a great deal of time ensuring they did not have to dole out charity to people from other parishes. Paupers seeking relief could be questioned by magistrates to find out where their home parish was, and pauper 'examination' papers often contain a potted history of the person in question, with date and place of work and employment history.

Justices of the Peace could order paupers to be sent back to their home parish, and 'removal orders' may include details of arrangements for the person's journey and any appeals against the process. Poor Law papers may be archived in quarter sessions, petty sessions, parish and Poor Law union records. Workhouse or poorhouse registers of admission and discharge may be in Poor Law union or board of guardian records.

A note on sensitive information: to protect people's privacy, records such as workhouse registers and coroners' files are closed for many years, usually 100 years or 75 years from the date filed. The same applies to school registers. Access depends on the archive's policy. School registers (for admissions as well as daily registers) may be held at your local archives or at the school. Some schools kept a daily log with the principal's comments on unusual occurrences.

County court files (sheriff courts in Scotland) may have claims lodged by sick or injured workers under the Workmen's Compensation Acts (1897 onwards). These records include the worker's name, address, details of his state of health and name and address of his employer.

When you first visit an archive or record office, you will be asked to register and sign the visitors' book. You will need a current reader's ticket or CARN (County Archives Research Network) ticket before you can view archival material. Most record offices are members of CARN and you can obtain a CARN ticket for use at any participating archive free of charge. A CARN ticket lasts for four years.

Proof of your identity with your name and permanent address is required for a CARN ticket, e.g. a driving licence, passport, bank statement, etc. Check the archive's policy before travelling. Sometimes an archive will request two passport-sized photos. Not all archives accept a TNA reader's ticket as identification without other supporting evidence.

Some archives such as Staffordshire and Stoke-on-Trent City Archives have their own separate registration service, although they may accept a CARN ticket as part identification to issue their own reader's ticket.

There is usually a charge for photocopying documents or making copies of those on microfilm/microfiche. Many archives like TNA now permit the use of digital cameras to photograph some original documents, but there may be a fee.

Always ask the archivist first or check the record office website's guidelines before using a camera. Flash photography is not permitted.

Most record offices have a searchable online catalogue but beware: cataloguing is an ongoing process. Only more recent acquisitions may be listed on the Internet, and you may need to visit the record office in person to locate older material not yet online which is still in card or paper catalogue indexes. Printed lists of canal holdings may be available from your county archivist.

Tip: some record office online catalogues do not work well with Internet Explorer. If you get repeated error messages or 'no results could be found' messages when searching online, try another web browser such as Mozilla Firefox.

Local Record Offices in England

Berkshire Record Office

Loveden papers relating to Thames and Severn Canal (D/ELV/B3-4) include toll accounts. Oxford Canal Co. minutes for 1785 (D/ESv/M/B9). Wilts & Berks Canal share certificates. Thames Conservancy (D/TC) papers. The Treacher papers (D/EX 1457/1) relating to the Thames Navigation include toll accounts, day work books, account books, etc. with workers' names. Register of Barges on the Thames Navigation in 1812 (D/EX 1457/1/130) has owner's name and address for each vessel. The health (canal boat) register for 1877–1914 is in the Reading Borough collection (R/RV1/1).

Berkshire Record Office, 9 Coley Avenue, Reading, Berkshire, RG1 6AF; www.berkshirerecordoffice.org.uk/; email: arch@reading.gov.uk; tel: 0118 937 5132.

Birmingham Archives and Heritage Service

Maps, plans and photographs. Birmingham Canal Navigation: mainly legal and financial papers and some relating to BCN boat register, early nineteenth century (MS 86) and (MS 626). Birmingham Canal Navigation and the Birmingham & Midland Canal Carrying Co. records for 1909–1982 (MS 856). Fellows, Morton & Clayton photographs, newspaper cuttings and maps (MS 454). Surveyors and estate agents Richard Fowler & Sons papers (MS20) includes material on several local canals.

Diary of wharfinger, carrier and boatbuilder G.R. Bird from 1820–1830 (662750). Holden family correspondence on canals (568603). The deed of settlement of the Birmingham Boat Company (1838) has the names of boatmen and builders who bought shares (MS 232/1).

Official Register of Boats and Inspections (MS 316) from 1879–1957: boat registers (9 vols, 1879–1960), inspection records (5 vols, 1934–1957) and Examining Officers' Reports (2 vols, 1912–1943). Chief Sanitary Inspectors' correspondence for 1935–1972 (MS 685).

Oral histories of boat children (MS 1497/13). Digbeth and Deritend local-history project 1989 (MS 1497).

Birmingham Archives and Heritage Service, Floor 6, Central Library, Chamberlain Square, Birmingham, B3 3HQ; http://calmview.birmingham.gov.uk/; email: archives.heritage@birmingham.gov.uk; tel: 0121 303 4549.

Bristol Record Office

Port of Bristol Medical Officer of Health sanitary reports on canal boats from 1885 onwards (33416).

Bristol Record Office, 'B' Bond Warehouse, Smeaton Road, Bristol, BS1 6XN; www.bristol.gov.uk/ccm/navigation/leisure-and-culture/records-and-archives/; email: bro@bristol.gov.uk; tel: 0117 922 4224.

Cheshire Archives and Local Studies

Deposited plans for the Bridgewater Canal (QDN 5), River Weaver papers (QDN 2), Mersey and Irwell Navigation (QDN 3), Manchester Ship Canal, Macclesfield Canal, etc. Registrar of Shipping and Seamen for Runcorn (NS). Port of Runcorn shipping records (NR).

Health (canal boat) register for Chester with index from 1879–1931 (ZD/DH). Runcorn health registers (LUR/57) for 1878–1949, register of complaints (LUR/58) for 1943–1961 and register of certificates (LUR/3928/6) for 1878–1966. Northwich health registers (LUNo 3897) for 1880–1940 including inspector's notebooks for 1937–1964 (LUNo 3897/7-9). Nantwich health registers (LUN 4452) for 1878–1924 and register of journal of canal-boat inspector (LRN/103) for 1914–1952. Canal boat-registration certificates issued by Stoke-on-Trent Registration Authority for North Staffs Railway Co. of Stoke-on-Trent (LNW/36).

The important River Weaver Navigation (LNW) series includes minute books, wage books, account books, registers of weighed flats (LNW4058) and wage records (D1361), etc.

Shropshire Union Railway and Canal Co. correspondence on pig-iron boatage (DDX 380). H.E. and H.J. Falk papers (D6917).

Cheshire Archives and Local Studies Service, Cheshire Record Office, Duke Street, Chester, Cheshire, CH1 1RL; www.cheshirewestandchester.gov.uk/ council_services/record_office.aspx; email: RecordOffice@cheshireshared services.gov.uk; tel: 0124 497 2574.

Chiswick Library Local Studies Service

Grand Junction Canal Co. letter book, boat register and certificates for 1889–1895 and 1903–1937. Brentford canal-boat inspection register (1879–1951), letter book and complaints book, inspection journal. List of barges owned by E.C. Jones registered with Port of London Sanitary Authority.

Chiswick Library Local Studies Service, Chiswick Library, Duke's Avenue Chiswick, W4 2AB; www.hounslow.info/libraries/chiswick/index.htm; email: localstudies-hct@laing.com; tel: 0208 994 1008.

Cumbria Record Office

Register of Canal Boats 1879 (WSMB/K1/9/Box 4).

Kendal County Offices, Kendal, LA9 4RQ; www.cumbria.gov.uk/ archives/default.asp; email: kendal.record.office@cumbriacc.gov.uk; tel: 0153 971 3540 or 0153 719 3539.

Derbyshire Record Office

Deposited plans (Q/RP) and quarter sessions records.

Erewash Canal: correspondence 1875–1879 (D382). Register of canal-boat inspections under the Canal Boat Acts from 1909–1946 (D5615); (D5615/1) includes the inspector's pocket book and journal. Ilkeston canal-boat registers for 1878–1942 (D4614).

Cromford Canal papers from 1781–1961 (D1954). Cromford Canal Toll Permit Book for 1838 (D6936) and navigation permits (D501) for 1814–1842 (incomplete series) (D501, D1041, D1265, D1366, D1391, D1534, D2652, D6936); permit books for 1821–1827 (D1265), navigation permits (D6559) for 1818–1839. Minutes of General Assemblies 1789–1852 (M689).

Collections D4614, D6936 and D501 all include the name of the vessel and master/owner, the type of goods carried, where loaded, where landed, weights, amounts paid, etc.

Chesterfield Canal: abstract of tonnages for 1774–1883 (D3200).

Derby Canal: permit receipt book, Sandiacre Area 1877–1878 (D995).

Nutbrook Canal: committee of proprietors minutes 1793–1872, 1947–1983, committee of proprietors annual general meetings minutes 1793–1954, book of entry of proprietors 1805–1948, No. 1 and No. 2 companies memorandum and articles of association, register of directors and secretaries, accounts, etc., 1925–1967. Nutbrook Canal Navigation copy minutes, register of members, accounts 1945–1981 (D3808); correspondence, papers, permits nineteenth–twentieth centuries (D517). Act for sale of canal and minutes of House of Lords committee, 1896 (D835) (D769, D995).

River Trent Navigation: copy of correspondence between Thomas Coke MP and Leonard Forsbrooke of Shardlow, 1699–1700 (D618).

Shardlow Boat Co. shipping register extracts for traffic on Trent & Mersey Canal 1831 (D603).

Derbyshire Record Office, Derbyshire County Council, County Hall, Matlock, DE4 3AG; www.derbyshire.gov.uk/leisure/record_office/default.asp; email: record.office@derbyshire.gov.uk; tel: 0162 953 9202.

Devon Record Office

Devon Record Office, Great Moor House, Bittern Road, Sowton, Exeter, EX2 7NL; www.devon.gov.uk/record_office.htm; email: devrec@devon.gov.uk; tel: 0139 238 4253.

Doncaster Archives

Thorne Rural District records (RD/THO) include a register of canal boats 1885–1957.

Doncaster Archives, King Edward Road, Balby, Doncaster, DN4 0NA; www.doncaster.gov.uk/leisure_in_doncaster/libraries/archives_local_stu dies/doncaster_archives.asp; email: doncaster.archives@doncaster.gov.uk; tel: 0130 285 9811.

Dudley Archives and Local Studies

Birmingham Canal Navigations land ledgers (Z123). The N. Hingley collection relating to canals (WRI/3/3) includes the BCN (WRI/3/3/1),

Shropshire Union Railway and Canal Co. (WRI/3/3/2) and other canal operators.

Dudley Archives and Local History Service, Mount Pleasant Street, Coseley, West Midlands, WV14 9JR; www.dudley.gov.uk/archives; email: archives.centre@dudley.gov.uk; tel: 0138 481 2770.

Gloucestershire Archives

Over 2,500 canal-related records. The British Waterways collection (D2460) and its earlier incarnations chiefly relates to the Gloucester & Sharpness Canal and the River Severn. It also holds Thames and Severn Canal (C/CTS) minute books, ledgers, cash books, wages books, correspondence, etc. Stroudwater Navigation Company (D1180), Gloucester & Berkeley Canal Co. (D2159), Canals and Tramroads Acts from the late eighteenth/ early nineteenth century, etc. Gauge book for trows, canal boats and barges on the River Severn in 1892 (D2460/2/1/12/24). Tolls and traffic records on the River Severn for 1836–1947 (D2460/2/1/12).

Canal-boat health registers from 1879–1952 (GBR/ L/6/13/3/).

A computer database of the health registers transcribed by the Friends of the National Waterways Museum can be viewed at the archive or via its online catalogue: series numbers GBR/L/6/13/3/1-6.

Search the Gloucestershire Genealogical Database by canal-boat inspections as well as name at http://ww3.gloucestershire.gov.uk/ genealogy/Search.aspx.

Gloucestershire Archives, Clarence Row, Alvin Street, Gloucester, GL1 3DW; www.gloucestershire.gov.uk/archives; email: archives@gloucestershire. gov.uk; tel: 0145 242 5295.

Hertfordshire Archives and Local Studies

Hoddesdon Canal Boats Register of Inspections for 1895–1897 (UDC/11/22) and Berkhamsted RDC canal-boats register of boats for 1911–1920 (RDC/2/37) and register of inspections for 1915–1927 (RDC/2/38), and certificates, inspections and Examining Officer's reports (various dates from 1901–1946): RDC/2/67/14.

Tring MOH's correspondence on canal boats 1877–1894 (LBH 3/4/20), Tring UDC Examining Officer's reports on canal boats 1917–1918 and list of numbers of boats registered each year 1922–1928 (UDC/18/133). Ware UDC's annual reports under the Canal Boats Acts and correspondence for 1886–1910 (UDC/19/9/1).

Hertfordshire Archives & Local Studies, Register Office Block, CHR 002, County Hall, Pegs Lane, Hertford, SG13 8EJ; www.hertsdirect.org/libsleisure/heritage1/HALS; email: hertsdirect@hertscc.gov.uk; tel: 0300 123 4049.

Hillingdon London Borough Local Heritage, Archives and Museums Service

Uxbridge register of canal boats for 1913–1951 and certificates of registration for 1941–1958 in the Uxbridge UDC Public Health Department records (O/UU/5/1).

Hillingdon Local Studies, Archives and Museums Service, Uxbridge Library, 14–15 High Street, Uxbridge, Middlesex, UB8 1HD; www.hillingdon. gov.uk/heritage; email: archives@hillingdon.gov.uk; tel: 0189 525 0702.

Hull History Centre

Records of the Associated British Ports and predecessors (C DPD).

Hull History Centre, Worship Street, Hull, HU2 8BG; www.hullhistory centre.org.uk/discover/hullhistorycentre.aspx; tel: 0148 231 7500.

Lancashire Record Office

Records for many different canals of the North West and beyond: maps, plans, accounts, minute books, correspondence, share certificates, photographic collection and much more. Parliamentary plans for canals and waterways (QDPC/C) for 1791–1952.

Returns of boats and barges in quarter session records (QDV) for 1795 onwards (QDV/16) includes return of vessels on the Bridgewater Canal (QDV 16/3). Series QDV/4 includes boats travelling from Sankey to St Helens, Sankey to Liverpool, Manchester, Bolton and Bury, Manchester to Stourport, Manchester to Birmingham, Manchester to Runcorn, Manchester to Wheelock, Worsley to Stone, Worsley and Manchester to Runcorn, and Manchester to Worsley.

Certificates of Canal Gauges QDD (Misc. Deeds) from 1790 onwards.

Journal of canal-boat inspections from 1929–1938 (RDLa 20/4). Miscellaneous papers relating to the Canal Boats Acts including report forms, draft report, 1931, notes, news cuttings, etc. regarding canal life and children on barges for 1877–1931 (RDL20/5).

BWB Canal Office records (DDX 1052) include wage and insurance books (DDX1052/2), maintenance records, e.g. workmen's job book for 1841–1845, reports on drownings, wages books, etc. (DDX1052/1).

Leeds and Liverpool Canal papers (DDBD/48). Manchester Ship Canal papers (DDBE, DDTR/12/2). Assignment of shares of flats and barges on the Douglas Navigation and Leeds and Liverpool Canal in 1776 (DDBb 1/1 and 2).

Lancaster Canal Co. records include property rentals, notices to quit tenancies, agreements for taking water for 1819, 1876–1892 (DDX 1298). Un-catalogued collection of Lancaster Canal Co. records includes shares, committee reports and annual reports, sketch plan, receipts, loan account, plan and report to Committee, 1793–1819 (DP 483, acc. 8652).

Rochdale Canal and Ashton Canal papers include minutes (DDHU/32). Peak Forest Canal permits for navigation of stone and limestone (Samuel Oldknow's boats) for 1805–1806 (DDX 199/12-13). The National Coal Board series has some records on canal dues and rents (NCAt/3/13), Manchester Ship Canal Co. (NCEv/8).

Workmen's Compensation Act files (CYBN/2) include canal workers.

A full list of canal papers is available.

Lancashire Record Office, Bow Lane, Preston, Lancashire, PR1 2RE; www.lancashire.gov.uk; email: record.office@lancashire.gov.uk; tel: 0177 253 3039.

Record Office for Leicestershire, Leicester and Rutland

An important canal collection; indexes are available. Deposited plans (QS72).

Enrolments under the Canal Acts (QS50) include Navigation Books (QS50/1) for 1794–1923.

The Curzon papers (DE1536) include Loughborough Navigation and Erewash Canal permits and related cargo receipts and accounts (DE1536/207B/3).

Acts of Parliament relating to canals in DG9, DE5099 and other collections.

Health (canal boat) registers for Hinckley Urban Sanitary Authority, including inspections, on microfilm MF594.

'Abstract of Canal Boats and Boat People in Leicestershire and Rutland in the Census 1841, 1851, 1861 and 1871' by J.R. Wignall (Library number L312, open shelf).

Record Office for Leicestershire, Leicester and Rutland, Long Street, Wigston Magna, Leicester, LE18 2AH; www.leics.gov.uk/record_office.htm; email: recordoffice@leics.gov.uk; tel: 0116 257 1080.

Lincoln Central Library

Journal of inspector of canal boats (L386) for 1906–1938.

www.lincolnshire.gov.uk/residents/discover-libraries/what-we-offer/lincoln-central-library.

Lincolnshire Archives

Lincoln City health department records include canal-boat reports and correspondence for 1929–1959. Lincoln City education files have papers on canal-boat children's school attendance. Gainsborough Poor Law Union School attendance records include correspondence on canal-boat children's education for 1900–1902 (PL/4/805/4/6).

Lincolnshire Archives, St Rumbold Street, Lincoln, LN2 5AB; www.lincolnshire.gov.uk/archives; email: lincolnshire.archives@lincolnshire.gov.uk; tel: 0152 278 2040.

Liverpool Record Office

Leeds and Liverpool Canal and Douglas Navigation papers (MD58) from the eighteenth and nineteenth centuries.

Health (canal boat) registers for boats on Leeds and Liverpool Canal (3004): 'Book 10' for 1923–1926 (3004/1/1), 'Book 12' for 1932–1938 (3004/1/2), 'Book 13' for 1938–1965 (3004/1/3). Inspector's lists of canal boats (3004/4) for 1907–1962. The Canal Boats public-health report (3004/8/5) for 1951–1964 has lists of vessels in the Liverpool area. Ledger with applications to register canal boats (3004/2) for 1936–1959. Daily statistics for boats registered and visited (3004/8/1) for 1953–1965. MOH reports to the Port Sanitary Authority for 1914–1974 include canal-boat inspections (352/4/ HEA).

NB Liverpool Record Office is closed until 2013; a temporary service is available. Check the website for updates to services.

Permanent address: Liverpool Record Office, Central Library, William Brown Street, Liverpool, L3 8EW; www.liverpool.gov.uk/Leisure_and_culture/ Libraries_and_archives/Catalogues_archive_and_local_history/index.asp; temporary service: www.liverpool.gov.uk/Leisure_and_culture/Libraries_ and_archives/index.asp; email: archives@liverpool.gov.uk; tel: 0151 233 5817.

London Metropolitan Archives

A vast collection with many canal-related papers including the Regent's Canal, Grand Junction Canal, etc. The CLA series includes the Thames Navigation and Thames Conservancy: canal-boat registers (CLA/ 037/PL/04). The Port of London Health Committee was responsible for inspecting canal boats (COL/CC/PLH). BWB engineers' records for the Lee Conservancy Board (ACC/2423).

London Metropolitan Archives, 40 Northampton Road, Clerkenwell, London, EC1R 0HB; www.cityoflondon.gov.uk/lma; email: ask.lma@ cityoflondon.gov.uk; tel: 0207 332 3820.

Greater Manchester County Record Office

Manchester Ship Canal Co. papers (B10) for 1884–1963 include minute books, staff records, accident books and fatal-accident registers, superannuation records, factory inspector reports, etc. Rochdale Canal Co. archive for 1790–1963 (ref. B2) includes minute books (B2/1/1/1-48) from the early 1790s to the 1930s, ledgers, journals, cash books, share records, letter books, etc. Mersey and Irwell Navigation/Bridgewater Canal records for 1779–1973 (M300) include minute books, engineer reports, toll traffic, share registers, staff records, etc.

Thomas Pickford of Manchester's papers, c.1815–1860 (M492).

Canal-boat inspector's records (M487) include registers (M487/1) for 1909–1961, journals (M487/2) for 1938–1972, and contraventions and cautions under the Canal Boats Acts for 1935–1964 (M487/3).

Guide to business records: www.gmcro.co.uk/Sources/UserGuide/ firms.html.

Greater Manchester County Record Office, 56 Marshall Street, New Cross, Manchester, M4 5FU; www.gmcro.co.uk; email: archiveslocalstudies@ manchester.gov.uk; tel: 0161 832 5284.

Norfolk Record Office

Canal Boat register (N/TC 51/43) for 1898–1952.

Norfolk Record Office, The Archive Centre, Martineau Lane, Norwich, Norfolk, NR1 2DQ; www.archives.norfolk.gov.uk/nroindex.htm, email: norfrec@norfolk.gov.uk; tel: 0160 322 2599.

Northamptonshire Record Office

Quarter session records (QS): deposited plans for Grand Junction/Grand Union, London and Birmingham Canals, Oxford and others.

Health (canal boat) registers for Daventry district including Braunston for 1879–1961, and journals of canal-boat inspectors for 1889–1942: MUS (D).

The George Freeston archive includes records from the Chief Engineer's office of the Grand Union Canal. These are un-catalogued and mainly consist of correspondence between 1902–1928 and 1941–1947. The Freeston collection also includes canal surveyors' account books for the Blisworth section 1849–1875, with wages for lock keepers and other canal employees: boxes 14 and 23.

Canal share certificates. The Ellesmere (Brackley) (E(B)) papers include canal account books and miscellaneous canal documents.

Northamptonshire Record Office, Wootton Hall Park, Northampton, NN4 8BQ; www.northamptonshire.gov.uk/en/councilservices/community/ ro/pages/default.aspx; email: archivist@northamptonshire.gov.uk; tel: 0160 476 2129.

North Yorkshire County Record Office

www.northyorks.gov.uk/archives.

Nottinghamshire Archives

Quarter Sessions deposited plans (C/QDU/DP/W). Prospectus plans for the Cromford, Nottingham, Grantham, Chesterfield and Erewash Canals (XC1-7 S) and Trent Navigation (XW2 L).

Chesterfield Canal Company memoranda, minute extracts, letters, etc. for 1805–1828 (DD 590/2-4). Cromford Canal Company (including Langley Mill) accounts for 1827 (DD 879/29). Grantham Canal Company, Grantham Canal passage notes for 1899–1916 (DD 389/1). Grantham Canal Navigation correspondence DD/2040/4.

Nottingham Canal Company accounts for 1797 (DD/E/35/10). Trent Navigation Co. vouchers for 1711–1819 (DD/33/1), and company report, stock issue; 1906–1907 (DD/TS/135/2/1-2). Trent Navigation Co. map of the Trent area in 1906–1907 (XW2 S). Trent Navigation Co. gauging tables (DD/NM/1) from 1856–1908 include boat builder, master, owner and previous owner for vessels. An (unnamed) canal-carrier account book (DD/2068/2).

Nottinghamshire Archives, County House, Castle Meadow Road, Nottingham, NG2 1AG; www.nottinghamshire.gov.uk/archives; email: archives@nottscc.gov.uk; tel: 0115 958 1634.

Salford Local History Library

Extensive Bridgewater Estates Collection (BW) from fifteenth–nineteenth centuries. Records of employees including wages, pensions and apprenticeship indentures (BW/A/5).

Readers wishing to access the collection are advised to check its catalogue via the A2A portal first and specify a catalogue number and the item they wish to view before contacting archivist Roseanne McLaughlin.

Salford Local History Library, Salford Museum and Art Gallery, Peel Park, The Crescent, Salford, M5 4WU; www.salford.gov.uk/lhlibrary.htm; email: local.history@salford.gov.uk and roseanne.mclaughlin@salford.gov.uk; tel: 0161 778 0814.

The Shakespeare Centre Library and Archive

Public Health Inspector Records (Stratford-upon-Avon Corporation) include canal-boat registers for 1879–1935 and canal inspector's journal (BRR 64/1-2).

The Shakespeare Centre Library and Archive, Henley Street, Stratford-upon-Avon, CV37 6QW; www.shakespeare.org.uk; email: scla@shakespeare.org.uk or records@shakespeare.org.uk; tel: 0178 920 4016 or 0178 920 1816.

Sheffield Archives

Canal-boat registers for the Sheffield Canal (SY/140/L1/) from 1878–1916. Sheffield City Council health department canal-boat regulation and registration records (CA 708/1-10) from 1878–1976. Two volumes of counterfoils of notices issued to boats contravening the Canal Boats Acts and Public Health Act of 1936 (CA 643). The Sheffield and South Yorkshire Navigation (SY/185/B3) papers from the 1960s include tonnage records and lock keepers' returns of boats passing through. The Fairbank collection (FC) of maps and surveys includes canals, and there are some late Georgian era canal papers in the Spencer Stanhope muniments (Sp. St.).

Sheffield Archives, 52 Shoreham Street, Sheffield, S1 4SP; www.sheffield.gov.uk/libraries/archives-and-local-studies; email: archives@sheffield.gov.uk; tel: 0114 203 9395.

Shropshire Archives

British Waterways (5465 series) papers for 1873–1986 include maps and plans. List of hours worked and labourers (Shropshire Union) for 1937–1950 (5465/905). LMSR Company list of workers' addresses and list of pensioners dated 1880 (5465/921). LNWR staff volume for 1920 (5465/922) – poor condition – ask the archivist. LMSR Shropshire Union section staff list dated 1938 (5465/923). Shropshire Union Office of Works journal of mechanics time sheet includes employees and wages (5687).

Ellesmere and Chester Canal Proprietors papers for 1844–1845 (1320).

Shropshire Archives, Shropshire Council Community Services, Castle Gates, Shrewsbury, SY1 2AQ; www.shropshire.gov.uk/archives.nsf; email: archives@shropshire.gov.uk; tel: 0174 325 5350.

Staffordshire and Stoke-on-Trent Archives

Offices at Stafford, Lichfield and Stoke-on-Trent.

http://www.staffordshire.gov.uk/leisure/archives/collections/Online Catalogues/GatewaytothePast/.

Stafford

Quarter sessions records include convictions for thefts from boats and other offences including boats. Brindley family papers (D538). James Brindley's order books and day books (Mf 79).

Staffordshire and Worcestershire Canal minutes and company clerk papers (D3186/1-9), canal permits issued at Great Haywood (D3900/1-2, 5967/1).

Complaint certificates under the Canal Boats Acts (D3766/1/4/6/2) for 1915–1934 for Cannock UDC. Canal-boat registration correspondence for 1955–1965 (D1526/1/126) for Stone UDC. Some documents such as D3766/1/4/6/2 and D1526/1/126 are stored offsite; notice required.

Staffordshire County Archives, Eastgate Street, Stafford, ST16 2LZ; www.staffordshire.gov.uk/leisure/archives; email: staffordshire.record.office@staffordshire.gov.uk; tel: 0178 527 8379.

Stoke-on-Trent City Archives

Canal-boat inspector's journal for Stoke-on-Trent from 1934–1969 (SD1127/1). Index cards for canal boats registered from 1896–1969 (SD 1127/2).

Basil Jeuda collection on the NSR (SD1288, D1415, SD1416).

Stoke-on-Trent City Archives, City Central Library, Bethesda Street, Hanley, Stoke-on-Trent, ST1 3RS; www.staffordshire.gov.uk/leisure/archives; email: stoke.archives@stoke.gov.uk; tel: 0178 223 8420.

Surrey History Centre

River Thames, Wey and Basingstoke Canal tonnage account for 1796–1812 (G85/2/4/1/43) and Wey Navigation list of barges, cargoes and charges for 1679–1680 (LM2026).
www.surreycc.gov.uk/surreyhistorycentre.

Walsall Local History Centre

Canal-boat register of inspection at Walsall (108/6) for 1905–1933 and register of inspection of canal boats (108/7) for 1924–1942. Volume of counterfoils of complaints under the Canal Boats Acts for 1912–1942 (347/58). Tipton Station (BCN) gauging registers of boats with owner details (164) for 1895–1944.

www.walsall.gov.uk/localhistorycentre.

Warwickshire County Record Office

The main canal collection is British Waterways series (CR1590) for the Ashby Canal, Oxford Canal, Coventry Canal, Grand Junction, Grand Union and others from 1791–1962. Records from Hatton and Hillmorton depots include printed forms relating to exemptions from military service with lists of canal employees 1916–1918 (CR1590/439). Lists of canal employees and their rates of pay 1946–1948 (CR1590/479). Engineers' wage books (CR1590/488-9), rent books (CR1590/492 and CR1590/1603), letters and copies of reports on accidents to boatmen and boatmen's wives for 1951–1959 (CR1590/1552-3), lock keepers' pay schedules and conditions for 1949–1955 (CR1590/1008). Many more records relating to staff.

Gauging tables for 1869–1891 (CR1590/529) and various dates (CR1590/543)

Canal-boat inspector's journal for Nuneaton from 1913–1937 (CR2418). Southam RDC canal-boat inspection book for 1921–1938 (CR1560/244). Canal-boat registration fee receipt book (includes names) for 1885–1925 (CR1618/W34/91).

Warwickshire County Record Office, Priory Park, Cape Road, Warwick, CV34 4JS; www.warwickshire.gov.uk/countyrecordoffice; tel: 0192 673 8959.

City of Westminster Archive Centre

Canal-boat registers in the Paddington registered district from 1900–1932 (1201/1), inspector's journal from 1928–1956 (1201/2), complaint form certificate book (1201/3.)

City of Westminster Archive Centre, 10 St Ann's Street, London, SW1P 2DE; www.westminster.gov.uk/services/libraries/archives/; email: archives@ westminster.gov.uk; tel: 0207 641 5180.

West Yorkshire Archive Service (WYAS)

The main archives are at Wakefield. There are four sister sites at Bradford, Calderdale (Halifax), Kirklees (Huddersfield) and Leeds. Readers should search the online database to ascertain the correct location for documents before travelling, and check if an appointment is required to view items.

Wakefield

Most canal holdings relate to British Waterways and canal companies which predated it. BW Northern Region collection (collection ref. C.299) has over fifty sub-series. The canal, navigation and company records include the Barnsley Canal Navigation (C299/2), Birmingham and Liverpool Junction Canal (C299/3), Calder and Hebble Navigation (C299/4), Chester Canal (C299/5), Huddersfield Canal Co. (C299/14), Leeds and Liverpool Canal Co. records (C299/16), Sheffield and S. Yorkshire Navigation (C299/30), Weaver Navigation (C299/37) and many others. C299 also includes the BWB Principal Engineer records from mid-nineteenth century–1972.

The largest collection is for the Aire & Calder Navigation (C299/1). Its records from 1919–1957 include details of boatmen with date of appointment/transfers, the boats they served on, record of disciplinary action or accidents while on duty. The date of birth is sometimes included, with date of leaving or death, especially if the boatmen died on their boat (C299/1/7/1/2).

Wakefield has canal-boat registers for Wakefield from 1878–1943, and Knottingley for 1948–1967, a volume of inspections and one of 'contraventions of regulations' for 1878–1965 (WWD5 (B185)). Aire & Calder Navigation records include wages for fly boat crews 1919–1957 (C299/1/7/1/2). Rent roll for the Ashton, Peak Forest and Macclesfield Canals (C299/57/6/5) and Lancaster Canal (C299/57/6/8) 1950s–1960s.

Calderdale

Calder and Hebble Navigation canal-boat register for 1793–1828 (HAS/B:6/11).

Kirklees Archive

Huddersfield canal-boat register for 1907–1920 (CBH/canal-boat register) stored off-site.

Bradford Central Library

Health register for Bradford for 1926–1941 (37D80).

West Yorkshire Archive Service, Registry of Deeds, Newstead Road, Wakefield, WF1 2DE; www.archives.wyjs.org.uk/wyjs-archives-service.asp; email: archives@wyjs.org.uk; tel: 0192 430 5980.

Bradford: www.archives.wyjs.org.uk/wyjs-archives-bradford.asp.
Calderdale: www.archives.wyjs.org.uk/wyjs-archives-calderdale.asp.
Kirklees: www.archives.wyjs.org.uk/wyjs-archives-kirklees.asp.
Leeds: www.archives.wyjs.org.uk/wyjs-archives-leeds.asp.
Wakefield: www.archives.wyjs.org.uk/wyjs-archives-wakefield.asp.

Wiltshire and Swindon History Centre

Wilts & Berks Canal records for 1796–1917 (2424) includes account books. Wilts & Berks Canal boat registers for 1878–1881 (2424/45). Canal-boat registers (Calne Borough Council) for 1878–1891 (G18/132/42) and 1885–1887 (G18/821/1). Kennet and Avon Canal registers of traffic passing through Semington Locks for 1879–1893 (1664) and time sheets for boats using the canal in 1886 (1644/14). Day book of maintenance on Kennet and Avon 1815–1827 (2940).

Wiltshire and Swindon Archives, Wiltshire and Swindon History Centre, Cocklebury Road, Chippenham, SN15 3QN; www.wshc.eu; email: archives@wiltshire.gov.uk; tel: 0124 970 5500.

Wolverhampton Archives and Local Studies

Canal-boat inspector's journal 1935–1965 (WOL-PH/1/6), canal-boat registers for 1882–1885 (DX-68), canal-boat registers for 1908–1938 (WOL-PH/1/1) and index (WOL-PH/1/2). Inspector of canal-boats register for 1959–1960 (WOL-D-MISC/1). Bilston canal-boat inspector's report book (C-UD-BIL/1/7/2/100). Wolverhampton Electricity Board records from

1916–1953 include files on gauging and weighing canal boats (DB-1/1-3) and correspondence on boatmen's wages (DB-1/4). Joseph Sankey & Son records include Midland Canal Boatmen's Wages Board welfare payments (DB-25).

Holt's index of boatmen and families (LS/L9292). Photographic collection you can view online.

Wolverhampton Archives and Local Studies, Molineux Hotel Building, Whitmore Hill, Wolverhampton, West Midlands, WV1 1SF; www. wolverhampton.gov.uk/leisure_culture/libraries/archives; email: archives@ wolverhampton.gov.uk; tel: 0190 255 2480.

Local Record Offices in Wales

Archives Wales

Electronic catalogue for archives in Wales. NB not all collections with Wales-related material are listed (e.g. TNA holdings are not included).

www.archivesnetworkwales.info.

National Library of Wales

The library holds baptisms, marriages and burials registers, bishops' transcripts, marriage bonds, Nonconformist records, wills and probate records, quarter sessions, Poor Law and education records, etc.

The National Library of Wales, Aberystwyth, Ceredigion, Wales, SY23 3BU; www.llgc.org.uk/; tel: 0197 063 2800.

Aberystwyth University

The university has a copy of a thesis by Caroline Jones, 'A Study of Inland Waterway Sources for Family History' (2007). The thesis is held at the Thomas Parry Library on the Llanbadarn Campus of the University. The item barcode is 1806048038 and shelf location is Thesis JON.

Library Support Services, Information Services, Hugh Owen Library, Penglais, Aberystwyth University, Aberystwyth, SY23 3DZ; www.aber. ac.uk/en/is/collections; email: libstore@aber.ac.uk; tel: 0197 062 2411.

Glamorgan Archives

Aberdare Canal Co. documents from late eighteenth century–early 1960s (DB). Quarter session records include Glamorganshire Canal accounts and Neath Canal other records (Q/D/G). The DART series includes Aberdare Canal and Glamorganshire Canal papers from the 1790s. Cardiff Borough records (BC) include Glamorganshire Canal records from 1791–1937.

Aberdare Local Board of Health (later Aberdare UDC): volume of canal-boat certificates of registration for November 1890–January 1891 (LBA/43) and canal-boat inspector's journal for 1890–1898 (LBA/44).

Glamorgan Archives, Clos Parc Morgannwg, Leckwith, Cardiff, CF11 8AW; www.glamro.gov.uk/; email: GlamRO@cardiff.gov.uk; tel: 0292 087 2200.

West Glamorgan Archive Service

Registry of shipping for Swansea (D/D PRO/RBS). Neath Canal Navigation Co. records (D/D NCa) includes accounts, tonnage books, wages, rent rolls, etc. Swansea Port Authority health records (PH1). Swansea Canal Navigation Co. records. Tennant Canal correspondence, letter books, accounting records, time books, tonnage books, shipping registers, deeds, etc. (DD/T).

West Glamorgan Archive Service, Civic Centre, Oystermouth Road, Swansea, SA1 3SN; www.swansea.gov.uk/westglamorganarchives; email: westglam.archives@swansea.gov.uk; tel: 0179 263 6589.

Neath Antiquarian Society

The Society's papers, which include Neath Canal Co. records for 1794–1881, can be consulted at the Neath Mechanics' Institute, 4 Church Place, Neath, SA11 3LL; tel: 0163 962 0139.

Abbreviations

BCN   Birmingham Canal Navigations
BWB   British Waterways Board
LMSR   London, Midland and Scottish Railway
LNWR   London and North Western Railway
NSR   North Staffordshire Railway
RDC   Rural District Council
UDC   Urban District Council.

WATERWAYS ARCHIVES AND OTHER SPECIALIST REPOSITORIES

Waterways Archives

The Waterways Trust administers the waterways archives at Ellesmere Port and Gloucester Docks; http://www.thewaterwaystrust.org.uk.

The Waterways Archive (Ellesmere Port)

This repository was formerly known as the David Owen Waterways Archive, and can still be found under that name on some websites.

Extensive collections on the Weaver Navigation Trust (BWWN), Middlewich Wharf and the Manchester Ship Canal. Charles Hadfield World Canals Research papers. Database of fleet lists for canal carrying companies such as Thomas Clayton of Oldbury Ltd. Parish register and census transcripts. Copies of health registers for Manchester (D7076), Nantwich (D1574), Chester (D7077), Runcorn (D7290), Northwich, Nantwich and Runcorn (D7502-4), and Liverpool (D7718/01-28). Ellesmere Port canal-boat inspector's journal. Kidderminster canal-boat inspector journals (E89/154). National Register of Archives (NRA) index for canals.

The Kitching collection (D7624, D7807, D7991) includes freight notes, toll checks boarding permits and correspondence for Middlewich wharf. Harecastle tunnel log book (D7074). Shropshire Union toll tickets (D7619). London and Midland Scottish Railway Co. declaration notes include boat name, captain, steerer's name and cargo carried (D1954). Anderton wage receipts (D0509) for the 1950s. North Staffordshire Railway Co. wages ledger (canals department) for 1850–1930 (20001.146).

Boatmen's name indexes and boat indexes. Oral histories of canal-company workers.

The Waterways Archive is located at the Boat Museum. Booking is required to visit the archive, which is normally open three days a week. Please give at least twenty-four hours' notice.

The Waterways Archive (Ellesmere Port), South Pier Road, Ellesmere Port, Cheshire, CH65 4FW; http://nwm.org.uk/TheWaterwaysArchive.html; email Linda Barley at: Linda.Barley@thewaterwaystrust.org.uk; tel: 0151 373 4378.

The Waterways Archive (Gloucester Docks)

British Waterways staff records (BW58) and wages, sick pay and pension details, house rents, etc. for the twentieth century. Register of accidents (BW58/4/4/3) from the early 1930s to the mid-1940s.

Grand Junction Canal (BW99), Grand Union Canal Co. (BW58), Trent & Mersey Canal (BW110). The Grand Union Canal records include Brentford and Paddington Toll Offices' traffic certificates and permits for the twentieth century (BW58/9). The Grand Junction Canal Co. records include barge and boat traffic, toll and gauging records for Brentford Lock (BW99/6). Staffordshire and Worcestershire Canal Navigation proprietors (BW151): correspondence, tolls and traffic, and canal maintenance notebooks.

Trent & Mersey Navigation (BW110): Records of the Company of Proprietors of the Navigation from the Trent to the Mersey: legal, financial and administrative records for 1762–1846, traffic records for 1799–1846, plans and surveys of the canal and lands belonging to the company for 1795–1836, records of Hugh Henshall & Co. for 1817–1845.

Canal-company minute books, e.g. the Wyrley and Essington Canal Navigation. Carriers, e.g. the Midland Canal Transport Ltd, Fellows, Morton & Clayton records (BW118) from 1879–1940s.

The archive has databases available for gauge registers including those belonging to the Birmingham Canal Navigations (BW165), Oxford Canal (BW162), Grand Junction Canal (BW99) and River Trent (BW98/2).

Canal-boat registers (health registers) for Hinckley, Leicester, Northampton and Birmingham (BW117). Sanitary inspectors' journals for the Coventry and Oxford Canals. Canal-boat inspectors' correspondence for Runcorn, Stoke-on-Trent, Tamworth, Towcester and other locations.

Certificates for boats with various sanitary authorities (BW117/4) including boats registered at Runcorn (BW117/4/7) from 1878–1852 with details of boats owned by the Bridgewater Navigation Co., Manchester Ship Canal Co., Messrs Potter & Son, William Bate & Co. and Richard Abel & Sons Ltd. Certificates for boats registered at Daventry from 1900–1944 (BW117/4/3), FMC boats registered at Uxbridge (BW117/4/10).

Reports on canal boats inspected at Runcorn Locks from 1915–1949 (BW117/6/1) include boats owned by the Manchester Ship Canal Co. (Bridgewater Dept), Mersey & Humber Carriers Ltd, Weaver Navigation Trustees and others.

The archive also has some records for Scottish canals, e.g. the Caledonian Canal (BW47) from 1887 to the mid-twentieth century, including some toll tables.

The archive has over 20,000 images and it is possible you may find a photograph of your ancestors or the boat or canal on which they worked. The photographic collection (BW192) can be searched online at the Virtual Waterways Archive Catalogue (see below), although images are not yet available to view on the web.

The Gloucester Docks archive is open to the public on weekdays. Booking is required to visit; please give a minimum forty-eight hours' notice.

The Waterways Archive (Gloucester Docks), Gloucester Research Service, 7th Floor, Llanthony Warehouse, The Docks, Gloucester, GL1 2EH; www.gloucesterwaterwaysmuseum.org.uk/museum.aspx; email Caroline Jones at: bwarchive@thewaterwaystrust.org.uk; tel: 0145 231 8224.

Virtual Waterways Archive Catalogue
This online resource gives the location of British Waterways and early canal-company documents in fifteen main repositories (including TNAS). The catalogue covers canal history from the seventeenth century to modern times for England, Wales and Scotland. You can search online for records kept by the partner repositories.

The website's family history section contains a series of articles on how to begin your research, and you can read the fascinating stories of four canal-boat families: www.virtualwaterways.co.uk/home.html; www.virtualwaterways.co.uk/Family_History_introduction.html.

Bodleian Library (University of Oxford) Special Collections
Oxford Canal Navigation accounts.

www.bodleian.ox.ac.uk/bodley/library/specialcollections.

British Library

The *Canal Boatmen's Magazine* for 1929–1932 (Shelfmark P.P.1090.c).

www.bl.uk; www.bl.uk/familyhistory.html.

Guildhall Library

The Library is now part of London Metropolitan Archives. The Company of Watermen and Lightermen records include registers of watermen, apprenticeship indentures, registers of barge owners, account books and cash books of barge owners' registration fees. The Sun Fire Office records include insurance papers for canal companies such as the Grand Junction Canal.

Guildhall Library, Aldermanbury, London, EC2V 7HH; www.cityof london.gov.uk/Corporation/LGNL_Services/Leisure_and_culture/Librar ies/City_of_London_libraries/guildhall_lib.htm; email: guildhall.library@ cityoflondon.gov.uk; tel: 0207 332 1868.

Institution of Civil Engineers

The Institution's Archives and Library has an important and extensive collection on canal and civil-engineering history, including engineers' reports and drawings. Account books. James Brindley's diaries for 1759–1763. Telford, Smeaton and Rennie correspondence. Charles Hadfield's research papers on William Jessop.

One of the largest collection of canal pamphlets in Britain. An appointment is needed to visit the archive.

Archivist Mrs Carol Morgan, Archives, Institution of Civil Engineers, 1 Great George Street, Westminster, SW1P 3AA; www.ice.org.uk/Library; email: archive@ice.org.uk or carol.morgan@ice.org.uk; tel: 0207 665 2043.

John Goodchild Collection

The Aldam manuscripts include documents on inland waterways such as the Rochdale Canal, Bradford Canal, Birmingham and Liverpool Junction Canal and others. The Leeds and Liverpool Canal papers include plans, company administration details, share certificates, information on employees on land, etc. Calder and Hebble Navigation manuscripts cover legal business, construction plans, employee information and so on.

View a summary of the collection holdings via A2A. This private collection can be consulted at the Local History Study Centre at the rear of the library in Drury Lane, Wakefield.

Local History Study Centre, Below Central Library, Drury Lane, Wakefield, WF1 2DT; www.wakefield.gov.uk/CultureAndLeisure/ HistoricWakefield/Investigate/WhereToGo/JohnGoodchild/default.htm; tel: 0192 429 8929.

John Rylands University Library
Extensive collection on waterways such as the Peak Forest Canal.

The largest collection of Methodist Connexional records in Britain is in the Methodist Archives and Research Centre (Methodist records of ministers, etc.).

Members of the public are permitted to visit the library three times, after which they must apply for external membership, for which there is a fee.

The John Rylands University Library, University of Manchester, Oxford Road, Manchester, M13 9PP; www.library.manchester.ac.uk/; tel: 0161 275 3751.

Labour History Archive (People's History Museum)
www.phm.org.uk/archive-study-centre.

Merseyside Maritime Museum Archive and Library, Liverpool
Liverpool shipping registers (C/EX) (formerly kept at Customs House). The registers include vessels registered at the port of Runcorn and those passing through Runcorn Dock. Indexes are available. The museum's website has many online guides.

Maritime Archives and Library, Merseyside Maritime Museum, Albert Dock, Liverpool, L3 4AQ; www.liverpoolmuseums.org.uk/maritime/ archive; tel: 0151 478 4499.

National Historic Ships
If you know the name of the boat on which your ancestor worked you can search the National Register of Historic Vessels (NRHV) and the National Archive of Historic Vessels (NAHV) online. More than 1,000

historic vessels are listed on the website. Over half of these vessels are privately owned or still in use. The website contains images, builder of each vessel (if known) and technical information for many vessels in its database. Your ancestor's boat will not be on the register if it was broken up, however!

National Historic Ships, Park Row, Greenwich, London, SE10 9NF; www.nationalhistoricships.org.uk; email: info@nationalhistoricships.org. uk; tel: 0208 312 8558.

National Maritime Museum
Manchester Ship Canal collection (MSC).

National Maritime Museum, Romney Road, Greenwich, London, SE10 9NF; www.nmm.ac.uk; online catalogue: www.nmm.ac.uk/collections/ archive/catalogue/; email: library@nmm.ac.uk; tel library: 0208 312 6516.

Nottingham University Library
Trent Navigation Co. records (RtN) for 1780–1934.

http://mssweb.nottingham.ac.uk/catalogue.

Salford City University Library
Duke of Bridgewater Archive (DBA) includes correspondence and payments books with wages for labourers on his canal.

www.library.salford.ac.uk/resources/special.

School of Oriental and African Studies (SOAS), University of London
The Council for World Mission (CWM) Archive includes London Missionary Society records for 1796–1966.

School of Oriental and African Studies, University of London, Thornhaugh Street, Russell Square, London, WC1H 0XG; www.soas. ac.uk/library; Archives and Special Collections Email: docenquiry@ soas.ac.uk; tel: 0207 898 4180.

University of Exeter Special Collections

Leeds and Liverpool Canal Company (MS 155).

http://as.exeter.ac.uk/library/about/special.

Wedgwood Museum Archives

The collection includes correspondence and workforce records.

www.wedgwoodmuseum.org.uk/visit/page/2199.

Miscellaneous

ARCHON

Directory of archives in Britain and those abroad with manuscript collections listed in the NRA index.

www.nationalarchives.gov.uk/archon/.

Archives Hub

Finding aid for locating archival material in educational and other specialist institutions.

www.archiveshub.ac.uk.

Black Country History

Explore repositories with information on Black Country people and places.

www.blackcountryhistory.org.

ARCHIVES AND FAMILY HISTORY HELP IN SCOTLAND

Explore holdings in Scottish archives at the Scottish Archive Network website at www.scan.org.uk.

The National Archives of Scotland (TNAS)

West Register House, TNAS

The records for transport industries (railways and canals) and businesses are kept at West Register House. Many BWB papers are still kept by British Waterways Scotland; a catalogue is available at West Register House.

Canal records are archived in the British Rail (BR), Ministry of Transport (MT) and British Waterways Board (BW) papers. Exchequer records (E) contain records of waterways (such as the Crinan Canal) cut through estates forfeited after the Jacobite rebellion. Maps and plans of projected canals and works can be found in the Register House Plans (RHP); legal disputes are in Court of Session and Sheriff Court records.

The BR series covers canal companies taken over by railways. Carlisle Canal minutes (BR/CCC). Caledonian Canal minutes and reports (BR/CCL) include engineer John Telford's letter book (BR/CCL/4/2). Crinan Canal papers (BR/CRI) include vessels and cargo traffic (BR/CRI/4). Edinburgh and Glasgow Union Canal minutes for 1813–1922 include accounts, tolls and charges, cash books, journals and ledgers (BR/EGU).

Forth and Clyde Canal records (BR/FCN) include a workmen's time book (BR/FCN/4/11) for Grangemouth Wet Dock and a notebook with lists of staff members (BR/FCN/4/10). Glasgow, Paisley and Johnstone Canal papers (BR/GPA).

The Ministry of Transport assumed responsibility for Scotland's canals in 1919. The MT series includes lock keepers' and workmen's wages for the Crinan Canal (MT 1/38). Canal tolls and licences for horse trackers on the Crinan and Caledonian canals (MT 1/253). The Exchequer series includes records for the Crinan Canal with monthly statements of 'canal dues' with details of vessels and cargoes (E331).

NB Some records for the Caledonian and Crinan canals are kept at TNA and the Gloucester Docks waterways archive.

The National Archives of Scotland, West Register House, 17a Charlotte Square, Edinburgh, EH2 4DJ; www.nas.gov.uk; guide to canal records and canal-company histories at TNAS: www.nas.gov.uk/guides/canal. asp; email: wsr@nas.gov.uk; tel: 0131 535 1400.

ScotlandsPeople Centre at TNAS

BMD certificates from 1855 onwards, old parish registers (1538–1854), Catholic registers, census returns, copies of wills and testaments (1513–1901) and more.

The Historical Search Room is used for researching family, local, national and international history.

ScotlandsPeople Centre, Room 28, New Register House, 3 West Register Street, Edinburgh, EH1 3YT; www.scotlandspeoplehub.gov.uk; email: enquiries@scotlandspeoplehub.gov.uk; tel: 0131 314 4300.

National Register of Archives for Scotland (NRAS)

A number of canal records, e.g. some Crinan Canal records such as minute books and Caledonian Canal toll books, diaries and other papers are still held in private collections, or owned privately but deposited in museums and libraries. Use the NRAS database to check the location of records and conditions of access.

www.nas.gov.uk/nras.

The National Library of Scotland

Rennie papers for Canals and Navigations for 1791–1821 (MS.19778-19785), Telford papers for 1805–1834 (MS.19969-19978), Crinan Canal correspondence and legal papers (MS.9500) and more, etc.

www.nls.uk.

Falkirk Council Archives

Falkirk Council Archives, Callendar House, Callendar Park, Falkirk, FK1 1YR; www.falkirk.gov.uk/services/community/cultural_services/museums/archives/archive.aspx; email: callendar.house@falkirk.gov.uk; tel: 0132 450 3779; guide to canal-company holdings including staff and workmen's records: www.falkirk.gov.uk/services/community/cultural_services/museums/archives/finding_aids/PDFs/business/canals.pdf.

Glasgow City Council Archives

Canal Boatmen's Institute and Port Dundas Mission (TD1301). Canal Boatmen's Institute nursery school register for 1943–1974 (D-ED7/36A) – restricted access.

Clyde Navigation Trust archive. View images from the archive's photographic collection online.

Archives and Special Collections, The Mitchell, North Street, Glasgow, G3 7DN; www.glasgow.gov.uk/en/Residents/Library_Services/The_Mitchell/Archives/; email: archives@glasgowlife.org.uk; tel: 0141 287 2910.

Scottish Association of Family History Societies

www.safhs.org.uk.

Scottish Genealogists Society

15 Victoria Terrace, Edinburgh, EH1 2JL; www.scotsgenealogy.com; email: enquiries@scotsgenealogy.com; tel: 0131 220 3677.

Free Census Scotland

www.freewebs.com/mmjeffery/index.htm.

ARCHIVES AND FAMILY HISTORY HELP IN IRELAND AND NORTHERN IRELAND

General Register Office for Northern Ireland

General Register Office for Northern Ireland, Oxford House, 49–55 Chichester Street, Belfast, BT1 4HL, Northern Ireland; www.nidirect. gov.uk/gro; email: gro.nisra@dfpni.gov.uk; tel: 0289 151 3101.

Public Record Office of Northern Ireland (PRONI)

Lagan Navigation Company records for 1796–1954 (COM/1). Returns of traffic and tolls include the Ulster Canal (COM/15/1), Coalisland Canal (COM/15/2), Newry Canal (COM/15/5), Lower Bann Canal (COM/15/4), Lagan Canal (COM/15/3), etc.

Family history guide: www.proni.gov.uk/index/family_history.htm.

The main genealogy sources are listed at: www.proni.gov.uk/index/family_history/family_history_key_sources.htm.

Search the will calendars and view digital images of copies of wills made in district registries on the PRONI website at www.proni. gov.uk/index/search_the_archives/will_calendars.htm; www.proni.gov. uk/index.htm.

Public Record Office of Northern Ireland, 2 Titanic Boulevard, Belfast, BT3 9HQ; www.proni.gov.uk; email: proni@dcalni.gov.uk; tel: 0289 053 4800.

Society of Genealogists Northern Ireland

Heather Flanders (Secretary), 280 Castlereagh Road, Belfast, BT5 6AD; www.sgni.net; email: secretary@sgni.net.

Genealogical Society of Ireland

General Secretary, Genealogical Society of Ireland, 11 Desmond Avenue, Dún Laoghaire, Co. Dublin, Ireland; www.familyhistory.ie.

General Register Office, Ireland

General Register Office, Government Offices, Convent Road, Roscommon, Ireland; www.groireland.ie; tel: +353 (0)906 632 900.

National Archives of Ireland

The Office of Public Works series includes the Grand Canal Company records (OPW10). Census returns for 1901 and 1911 and transcripts of some earlier census returns.

Online guide to the OPW series has series references for some employment records: www.nationalarchives.ie/topics/OPW/opw.html.

Guide for finding parish registers for different denominations in Ireland: www.nationalarchives.ie/genealogy/church.html.

Guide to the location of wills in Ireland and Northern Ireland: www.nationalarchives.ie/genealogy/testamentary.html.

1901 and 1911 censuses (free): www.census.nationalarchives.ie.

The National Archives, Bishop Street, Dublin 8, Ireland; www.national archives.ie; email: mail@nationalarchives.ie; tel: + 353 (0)14 072 300.

National Library of Ireland

Roman Catholic parish registers, land valuations, trade and social directories, estate records and newspapers.

National Library of Ireland, Kildare Street, Dublin 2, Ireland; www.nli.ie; email: info@nli.ie; tel: +353 (0)16 030 200.

Representative Church Body Library of Ireland

Braemor Park, Churchtown, Dublin 14, Ireland; www.library.ireland. anglican.org; tel: + 353 (0)14 923 979; email: library@ireland.anglican.org.

Irish Family History Foundation

www.rootsireland.ie.

C

FAMILY HISTORY HELP IN ENGLAND AND WALES

General Register Office (England and Wales)
Birth, marriage and death certificates for England and Wales from 1 July 1837 onwards.

General Register Office Certificate Services Section, General Register Office, PO Box 2, Southport, PR8 2JD; www.gro.gov.uk/gro/content/certificates/default.asp; email: certificate.services@ips.gsi.gov.uk; tel: 0845 603 7788.

Principal Registry of the Family Division (Probate Service)
www.hmcourts-service.gov.uk/infoabout/civil/probate/index.htm.

Guide to obtaining copies of probate records in England and Wales: www.hmcourts-service.gov.uk/cms/1226.htm.

Family History Societies

Federation of Family History Societies

www.ffhs.org.uk; email: info@ffhs.co.uk; tel: 0145 520 3133.

Society of Genealogists

Society of Genealogists, 14 Charterhouse Buildings, Goswell Road, London, EC1M 7BA; www.societyofgenealogists.com; www.sog.org.uk/index.shtml; email: membership@sog.org.uk; tel: 0207 251 8799.

Canal Family History

Coventry Family History Society

Online searchable canal-boat (health) register for some masters and owners of boats working the Coventry Canal from late 1870s to the 1930s.

Membership Secretary, Coventry Family History Society, 13 Clayton Road, Coventry, CV6 1FD; www.covfhs.org; www.covfhs.org/Content/DataCanal.php; email: enquiries@covfhs.org.

Bedford Canal Workers in 1861 Census (Linslade)

www.bedfordshire.gov.uk/CommunityAndLiving/ArchivesAndRecord Office/CommunityArchives/Linslade/CanalWorkersInThe1861Census. aspx.

EurekA Partnership

The partnership has transcribed and published family history material including Nonconformist registers for the counties of Bedfordshire, Berkshire, Buckinghamshire, Gloucestershire, Northamptonshire, Oxfordshire, Surrey, Warwickshire and Worcestershire.

Transcripts of canal-boat inspectors' books for the Oxford Canal (Lower Heyford) and the boat register for the Oxford Regional Authority. Canal-boat inspectors' books and boat register for the Grand Junction Canal at Daventry. Canal-boat register for the Droitwich Registration Authority. Register and canal-boat inspector's journal for the Stratford-upon-Avon Canal. Also transcripts of the register of boats (1795) for Warwickshire, and for the River Thames and Basingstoke Canal.

19A Station Road, Stoke Mandeville, Aylesbury, Bucks, HP22 5UL; www.eurekapartnership.com/index.htm; www.eurekapartnership.com/page18.htm.

Leeds and Liverpool Canal Boat Families

The Ormskirk & District Family History Society has created a boat-families website as an aid for researchers with ancestors on the Leeds and Liverpool Canal and other south-west Lancashire waterways. There's an online index of family names from the late eighteenth century onwards. A database on CD-ROM of boatmen and families in Burscough and the surrounding area is available.

Ormskirk & District Family History Society, PO Box 213, Aughton, Ormskirk, Lancashire, L39 5WT; www.odfhs.org.uk; www.boatfamilies. org.uk; email: boatfamilies@odfhs.org.uk.

Lincolnshire Family History Society

The Society has published a CD-ROM: 'Boatmen & boat owners from the Lincoln City Boat Register (1795), Lindsey Boat Register (1795) and Lincoln City reports on Canal Boats'.

www.lincolnshirefhs.org.uk/index.htm; email: secretary@lincolnshirefhs. org.uk.

Northamptonshire Family History Society

The society has publications on boat people working on the Oxford and Great Junction canals, Stoke Bruerne and Braunston, as well as Colin Chapman's *Tracing Ancestors in Northamptonshire* (Lochin Publishing, 2000).

Membership Secretary: Mr Ivor Watson, 7 Centre Parade, Kettering, Northants, NN16 9TL; www.northants-fhs.org; email: membership@ northants-fhs.org; tel: 0153 639 2059.

Northamptonshire Families

These databases compiled by Norman Tew include the parishes of Stoke Bruerne and Blisworth.

www.tech2u.com.au/~normtew/index.htm;
www.tech2u.com.au/~normtew/sbn/;
www.tech2u.com.au/~normtew/blis/index.htm.

Northamptonshire Surnames List

www.kellner.eclipse.co.uk/genuki/NTH/Surnames.

Nottinghamshire Family History Society

www.nottsfhs.org.uk.

Stoke-on-Trent Waterways and Canals

www.thepotteries.org/waterways/index.htm.

Warwickshire 'Strays'

A list compiled by Maureen Surman of boatmen in censuses from 1841–1891 at Worcester Wharf, Birmingham.

www.genuki.org.uk/big/eng/WAR/CanalStrays.html.

Wirksworth Parish Records 1600–1900

Database of canal boatmen and workers on the Cromford Canal compiled by John Palmer from the 1841 census.

www.wirksworth.org.uk/Index.htm;
www.wirksworth.org.uk/X460.htm#census.

Wolverhampton Boatmen

Holt's Index is a database of Wolverhampton boats, boaters and their families, collated from parish registers by Norman Holt. Copies are available at the waterways archives, or you can download the documents from the London Canal Museum website at www.canalmuseum.org.uk/collection/holts.htm, or view the index here at www.genuki.org.uk/big/eng/STS/Names/WolvCanal.html.

Wolverhampton Parish Register Indexes

Indexes searchable online by name or occupation (NB not a complete collection of Wolverhampton registers).

www.wolverhamptonhistory.org.uk/resources/indexes.

Cyndi's List of Canals, Rivers and Waterways Websites

www.cyndislist.com/canals.htm.

Free Rootsweb Genealogy Mailing List (Canal People)

http://lists.rootsweb.ancestry.com/index/other/Occupations/CANAL-PEOPLE.html.

Jim Shead's Family History Page

This has helpful hints.

www.jim-shead.com/waterways/mwp.php?wpage=FamilyHistory.htm.

John Roberts Waterways Index

An ever-growing database of boatmen, boats, canal workers on the land and family history information. If you have a query you hope may be answered from the index please send a stamped addressed 9in by 4in envelope with your query to Mr John Roberts, 52 St Andrew's Road, Sutton Coalfield, West Midlands, B75 6UH. Donations and further information for adding to the index are welcomed.

Railway Ancestors Family History Society

The society's journals include canals associated with railways.

www.railwayancestors.org.uk.

Rivers and Other Waterways

A comprehensive study of family history resources for river boatmen, watermen and lighter men is beyond the scope of this book. However, the following may be of interest.

Welcome to the Bargemen

This impressive website is a good launching point for tracing ancestors who worked on the Thames sailing barges and docks along this great river. Also includes Norfolk and Suffolk river boatmen. Indexes for boatmen.

www.bargeman.co.uk.

Waterman's Hall, London

Family history help for watermen and lightermen on the River Thames.

The Watermen's Company, 16–18 St-Mary-at-Hill, London, EC3R 8EF; www.watermenshall.org; www.watermenshall.org/tracing-ancestors; email: admin@watermenshall.org (family history research enquiries); tel: 0207 283 2373.

General Family History Websites
Ancestry: www.ancestry.co.uk
Cornucopia: www.cornucopia.org.uk/html
Family Relatives: www.familyrelatives.com
Find My Past: www.findmypast.com
The Genealogist: www.thegenealogist.co.uk
Genes Reunited: www.genesreunited.co.uk
Family Search (Latter-Day Saints): www.familysearch.org/eng/default.asp
Origins Network: www.origins.net.

Census Records, BMDs, etc.
UK Census Online censuses from 1841 to 1901 (free search, pay to view): www.ukcensusonline.com
1911 Census (free search, pay to view): www.1911census.co.uk
Free UK Census: www.freecen.org.uk
Free UK BMDs: www.freebmd.org.uk
Free Reg (parish and Nonconformist registers): www.freereg.org.uk
Nonconformist and Non-Parochial BMD records: www.bmdregisters.co.uk
Collections of early parish registers to view for free including Warwickshire: www.archive.org.

D

CANAL AND TRANSPORT SOCIETIES AND WEBSITES

Canal History and Heritage Societies

Boat Museum Society

Membership Secretary, Boat Museum Society, The National Waterways Museum, Ellesmere Port, Cheshire, CH65 4FW; www.boatmuseum society.org.uk/index.html; list of boat societies: www.boatmuseum society.org.uk/links.html#boatsoc; email: volunteers@boatmuseumsociety. org.uk.

Inland Waterways Association

This charity, first founded in 1946, campaigns for the preservation and restoration of Britain's inland waterways. The Association has several regional branches.

IWA, Island House, Moor Road, Chesham, HP5 1WA; www. waterways.org.uk; email: iwa@waterways.org.uk; tel: 0149 478 3453.

Inland Waterways Association of Ireland (IWAI)

Brenda Ainsworth, IWAI Membership Secretary, 25 Ellesmere Avenue, North Circular Road, Dublin 7, Ireland; www.iwai.ie; tel: 0283 832 5329.

Royal Yachting Association Scotland

The Association represents inland boaters following the Scottish IWA's closure.

Caledonia House, 1 Redheughs Rigg, South Gyle, Edinburgh, EH12 9DQ; www.ryascotland.org.uk; email: admin@ryascotland.org.uk; tel: 0131 317 7388.

Railway & Canal Historical Society

The Railway & Canal Historical Society includes regional and special interest groups. Their website has a comprehensive list of links to archives, collections, libraries and museums.

General enquiries: Hon. Secretary, Mr M. Searle, 3 West Court, West Street, Oxford, OX2 0NP; Membership Secretary: Mr R.J. Taylor, 16 Priory Court, Berkhamsted, HP4 2DP; www.rchs.org.uk.

The Waterways Trust

The Waterways Trust, Llanthony Warehouse, Gloucester Docks, Gloucester, GL1 2EH; www.thewaterwaystrust.org.uk; tel: 0145 231 8220.

The Waterways Trust Scotland

The Waterways Trust Scotland, New Port Downie, Lime Road, Tamfourhill, Falkirk, FK1 4RS; www.thewaterwaystrust.org.uk/scotland. shtml; tel: 0132 467 7822.

Canal and Boat Preservation Societies

Historic Narrow Boat Owners Club

The Society actively campaigns for the preservation of canal heritage. The website has information on historic canal vessels.

Membership Secretary: David Daines, 40 Hazell Road, Farnham, Surrey, GU9 7BP; www.hnboc.org.uk; email: MemSec@hnboc.org.uk; tel: 0125 272 4811.

Horseboating Society

Horseboating Society Membership, c/o 7 Carlisle Close, Winsford, Cheshire, CW7 2LH; www.mossley.freeuk.com/horseboating; membership email: walter.lucey@btinternet.com; tel chairperson, Sue Day: 0145 783 4863.

Narrow Boat Trust

Membership Secretary: Gill Clutterbuck, 1 Starmount Cottages, Old Horsham Road, Beare Green, Dorking, Surrey, RH5 4QY; www.narrow boattrust.org.uk; email: gill.clutterbuck@homecall.co.uk; tel: 0130 671 1708.

Wooden Canal Boat Society

Aims to restore and preserve old wooden working boats.

Wooden Canal Boat Society, 173 Stamford Street, Ashton-under-Lyne, OL6 7PS; www.wcbs.org.uk; tel: 0161 330 8422.

Canal History and General Websites

Canal Archive: Bridging the Years

This project from Salford City Archives and Trafford Metropolitan Borough Council tells the stories of the Bridgewater Canal and Manchester Ship Canal using illustrations, maps and video clips.

www.canalarchive.org.uk.

Canal Junction

Information on present-day canals, boats, holidays, etc. as well as history and heritage. The site has links to the many canal and restoration societies in Britain.

www.canaljunction.com/index.html;
www.canaljunction.com/canal/heritage.htm;
www.canaljunction.com/canal/society.htm.

David Kitching's Canal History

www.brocross.com/canal/canal.htm.

Historic Narrow Boats Working Boats Directory

www.workingboats.org.uk.

Mike Clarke's Canal History

www.mikeclarke.myzen.co.uk/canals.htm.

Jim Shead's Waterways Information

Vast waterways resource brimful of information.

www.jim-shead.com/waterways/index.php.

Richard Thomas's History of Steam Driven Narrow Boats

www.steamershistorical.co.uk/steamers_home.htm.

Navvyman

Dick Sullivan's book, first published by Coracle Press in 1983, tells the stories of canal and railway navvies.

www.victorianweb.org/history/work/sullivan/contents.html.

Miscellaneous
Canal Guide: www.canalguide.co.uk
Commercial Boat Operators Association: www.cboa.org.uk
George's Canal Boating in the UK and Europe: www.canals.com/index.htm
UK Canals Network has a list of canal preservation societies: www.ukcanals.net/cansoc.html
Wild Over Waterways helps adults and children explore waterways heritage and enjoy the waterways safely: www.wow4water.net.

E

EARLY REGISTERS OF BOATS AND BARGES

The 1795 registers are usually archived in quarter sessions records at your local record office. Contact details for archives listed here are in Section B2. There are some early registers relating to river navigations not listed here; check your local record-office catalogue.

Berkshire Record Office
List of vessels on the navigation from Newbury to London and from Marlow to London (lists twelve vessels giving name, burthen, master and number of crew) (Q/RPA/1/11).

Bristol Record Office
Register of ships for 1795–1802 (05077).

Cheshire Archives and Local Studies
Quarter sessions series (QDN) has registers of vessels for 1795–1812 (QDN4) including registration applications.

Derbyshire Record Office
Register of boats and barges from 1795–1799 (Q/RM/3/1).

Devon Record Office
Register of barges on the Exeter, Stover and Hackney canals and some coasting vessels (QS/70/1).

Doncaster Archives
Registers of vessels for 1795–1803 on the River Don Navigation: Tinsley to Goole, and from Goole to York, Hull and Gainsbrough (AB5/2/144-8).

Gloucestershire Archives
Register of canal boats and barges (Q/RR/1).

Hull History Centre
Registers of canal boats (C BRE/3).

Lancashire Record Office
Returns of Boats and Barges (QDV/16) including vessels on the Bridgewater Canal (QDV 16/3).

Record Office for Leicestershire, Leicester and Rutland
Register of Inland Navigation Boats and Barges (QS49).

Lincolnshire Archives
Boat Register Book for 1795–1807 (LQS/D/8).

London Metropolitan Archives
Barge-registration certificates for the Thames (MJ/SP/1795).

Norfolk Record Office
Registry of Keels for 1795–1798 (Y/C/38/3).

North Yorkshire County Record Office
River craft register for 1795–1799 is for vessels travelling to and from New Malton in the North Riding (QDR).

Staffordshire and Stoke-on-Trent Archives
Stafford Record Office has boat and barge registers (Q/Rub).

Surrey History Centre
Register of barges for 1795–1807 (QS6/2/1) and certificates of barges for 1795–1797 (with a list) on River Thames (QS6/2/2).

Warwickshire County Record Office
Registers of boats, barges and other vessels for 1795–1796 (QS/95/4-9).

F
PLACES TO VISIT

The three National Waterways Museums in England are at Ellesmere Port, Gloucester Docks and Stoke Bruerne.

The National Waterways Museum, Ellesmere Port
The Ellesmere Port site was once a bustling canal dock; many of its industrial Victorian buildings still survive. Climb aboard narrow boats and barges, and learn more about the social history of the canals.

National Waterways Museum, South Pier Road, Ellesmere Port, Cheshire, CH65 4FW; www.nwm.org.uk; email: ellesmereport@thewaterwaystrust.org.uk; tel: 0151 355 5017.

Gloucester Waterways Museum
Visit the boat collection, explore the Propulsion Gallery and watch videos of canal workers.

Gloucester Waterways Museum, Gloucester Docks, Llanthony Warehouse, The Docks, Gloucester, GL1 2EH; www.gloucesterwaterways museum.org.uk/default.aspx; email: gloucester@thewaterwaystrust.org.uk; tel: 0145 231 8200.

The Canal Museum, Stoke Bruerne
The Stoke Bruerne museum is housed in a restored corn mill by the Grand Junction Canal; the famous Blisworth tunnel is a short walk away.

Canal Museum, Stoke Bruerne, near Towcester, Northants, NN12 7SE; www.stokebruernecanalmuseum.org.uk; email: stokebruerne@thewater waystrust.org.uk; tel: 0160 486 2229.

Anderton Boat Lift, Cheshire

This engineering marvel was built in 1875 to transfer boats and their cargoes between the Trent & Mersey Canal and the Weaver Navigation. It was restored by British Waterways to working order in 2002.

Anderton Boat Lift, Lift Lane, Anderton, Northwich, Cheshire, CW9 6FW; www.andertonboatlift.co.uk; email: info@andertonboatlift.co.uk; tel: 0160 678 6777.

Banbury Museum

Waterways gallery and historic working boatyard on the Oxford Canal.

Banbury Museum, Spicehall Park Road, Banbury, Oxon, OX16 2PQ; www.cherwell.gov.uk/banburymuseum; tel: 0129 575 3752.

Basingstoke Canal Visitor Centre

Mytchett Place Road, Mytchett, Surrey, GU16 6DD; www.basingstoke-canal.co.uk; email: info@basingstoke-canal.co.uk; tel: 0125 237 0073.

Black Country Living Museum

Interesting canal-side area with historic boats and a reconstructed building made from the timbers of an old narrow boat.

Black Country Living Museum Trust, Tipton Road, Dudley, West Midlands, DY1 4SQ; www.bclm.co.uk; email: info@bclm.co.uk; tel: 0121 557 9643.

Etruria Industrial Museum

The last steam-powered potters' mill in Britain. It hosts a yearly canal-side festival.

Etruria Industrial Museum, Lower Bedford Street, Etruria, Stoke-on-Trent, ST4 7AF; www.stokemuseums.org.uk/eim; email: etruria@stoke.gov.uk; tel: 0178 223 3144.

Foxton Inclined Plane, Leicestershire

Historic boat lift opened in 1900 to speed up boat traffic at Foxton. The museum tells the story of the lift and the boat people who used it. There are plans to restore the lift. The Old Union Canals Society has an archive at the museum.

Foxton Inclined Plane Trust, Foxton Canal Museum, Middle Lock, Gumley Road, Foxton, Leicestershire, LE16 7RA; www.fipt.org.uk; email: info@fipt.org.uk; tel: 0116 279 2657.

Falkirk Wheel

Modern 'rotating' boat lift (built 2002) to connect the Forth and Clyde Canal with the Union Canal.

The Falkirk Wheel, Lime Road, Tamfourhill, Falkirk, FK1 4RS; www.thefalkirkwheel.co.uk; email: info@thefalkirkwheel.co.uk; tel: 0870 050 0208.

Galton Valley Canal Heritage Centre

Galton Valley Canal Heritage Museum, Brasshouse Lane, Smethwick, B66 1BA; www.laws.sandwell.gov.uk/ccm/navigation/leisure-and-culture/museums-and-galleries/our-museums/galton-valley-canal-heritage-centre/; email: museumarts_tourism@sandwell.gov.uk; tel: 0121 558 8195.

Kennet and Avon Canal Trust Museum

Kennet and Avon Canal Trust, Couch Lane, Devizes, SN10 1EB; www.katrust.org; email: archiveadmin@katrust.org.uk; tel: 0138 072 1279.

Linlithgow Union Canal Centre

There's a canal centre to visit, and there are plans to put a database of boat masters of the Linlithgow Union Canal online.

Linlithgow Union Canal Society, Manse Road Basin, Linlithgow, West Lothian, EH49 6AJ; www.lucs.org.uk; museum website (under construction): www.museum.lucs.org.uk/; tel: 0150 667 1215.

London Canal Museum

12–13 New Wharf Road, London, N1 9RT; www.canalmuseum.org.uk; tel: 0207 713 0836.

Museum of the Broads

This museum, dedicated to the heritage of the Norfolk and Suffolk Broads, has an archive and photographic collection.

The Museum of the Broads, The Staithe, Stalham, Norfolk, NR12 9DA; www.northnorfolk.org/museumofthebroads/default.asp; email:info@ museumofthebroads.co.uk; tel: 0169 258 1681.

Rickmansworth Waterways Trust

Batchworth Lock Canal Centre, 99 Church Street, Rickmansworth, Herts, WD3 1JD; www.rwt.org.uk; email: enquiries@rwt.org.uk; tel: 0192 377 8382.

Powysland Museum and Montgomery Canal Centre

Powysland Museum, The Canal Wharf, Welshpool, Powys, SY21 7AQ; www.powyslandclub.co.uk/museum.htm; www.powys.gov.uk/index.php; tel: 0193 855 4656.

Shardlow Heritage Centre

Canalside, London Road, Shardlow, Derby, DE72 2GA; http://homepages. which.net/~shardlow.heritage; email: shardlow.heritage@which.net.

Waterways Ireland Visitor Centre

Waterways Ireland Visitors Centre, Grand Canal Quay, Dublin 2, Ireland; www.waterwaysireland.org/index.cfm/section/article/page/Waterway sIrelandVisitorCentre; email: info@waterwaysireland.org; tel: +353 (0)16 777 510.

Yorkshire Waterways Museum

The Yorkshire Waterways Museum, Dutch River Side, Goole, DN14 5TB; www.waterwaysmuseum.org.uk; email: info@waterwaysmuseum.org.uk; tel: 0140 576 8730.

SELECT BIBLIOGRAPHY

Contemporary Sources
Newspapers and official publications as mentioned in the text:

Commercial Directory for Cheshire, Pigot & Co. (1822–3)

Eighteenth Annual Report of the Local Government Board 1888–9 (1889)

Fifteenth Report of the Commissioners for Making and Maintaining the Caledonian Canal, X (1818)

Fourteenth Annual Report of the Local Government Board 1884–5 (1885)

Legal Observer or Journal of Jurisprudence Vol. XVIII, May to October 1839 (Edmund Spettigue, 1839)

Mechanics' Magazine, Museum, Register, Journal, and Gazette Vol. XVII (London, 1832)

Mechanics' Magazine, Museum, Register, Journal, and Gazette Vol. XIX (London, 1833)

New Monthly Magazine and Universal Magazine Part II (London, 1820)

New Statistical Account of Scotland Vol. VII (William Blackwood & Sons, 1835)

Report from His Majesty's Commissioners … into … Practical Administration of the Poor Laws, Appendix E: Vagrancy (44) (1834)

Report from the Select Committee into … the Practice of Carrying Goods and Merchandise on Canals, Navigable Rivers, and Railways on Sundays, XXI (1841)

Report of the Commissioners into the … Factory and Workshops Acts Vol. 1, Appendix C, XXIX (C.1443) (1876)

Report of the Select Committee on the Canal Boats Act (1877) Amendment Bill, 263 (1884)

Reports of the Inspectors of Factories, half year ending 30 April 1874 (1874)

Reports of the Inspectors of Factories, half year ending 31 October 1875 (1876)

Second Report of the Commissioners appointed to recommend and consider a General System of Railways for Ireland, XLVII Part 1 (1838)

Sixth Report of the Inspectors appointed … to visit the Prisons of Great Britain: Northern and Eastern District (339), V (1841)

Adolphus, John, *Political State of the British Empire Vol. III* (T. Cadell & W. Davies, 1818)

Boswell, James (ed.), *Scots Magazine Vol. XXXVI* (Edinburgh, 1774)

Cleland, James, *The Rise and Progress of the City of Glasgow* (Glasgow, 1820)

Cooke, George Alexander, *Topographical and Statistical Description of Staffordshire* (c.1803)

De Salis, Henry, *A Chronology of Inland Navigation* (E. & F.N. Spon Ltd, 1897)

Dugdale, James, *The New British Traveller or English Panorama of England and Wales*, Vol. 2 (London, 1819)

Gell, R. and Bradshaw, T., *The Gloucestershire Directory* (Gloucester, 1820)

Hassell, John, *A Tour of the Grand Junction Canal* (London, 1819)

Head, Sir George, *A Home Tour through the Manufacturing Districts of England* (John Murray, 1836)

Healy, Samuel, 'Steam Power on the Grand Canal Ireland', Forrest, James (ed.), *Minutes of the Proceedings of the Institution of Civil Engineers*, Vol. 26 (London, 1867)

Hemingway, Joseph, *History of the City of Chester* (2 vols, Chester, 1831)

Hollingshead, John, *Odd Journeys In and Out of London* (Groombridge & Sons, 1860)

Mayo, John J., *Mercantile Navy List and Maritime Directory for 1867* (London, n.d.)

Partington, Charles F., 'Canals of Great Britain', *British Cyclopaedia of Arts, Sciences, History, Geography, Natural History and Biography Vol. I* (W.S. Orr & Co., 1838)

Pennant, Thomas, *Journey from Chester to London* (London, 1811)

Pennington, Myles, *Railways and Other Ways* (Williamson & Co., Toronto, 1894)

Pitt, William, *Topographical History of Staffordshire* (Newcastle under Lyme, 1817)

Robertson, J. (ed.), *Mechanics Magazine, Museum, Register, Journal and Gazette Vol. XLI* (London, 1844)

Robins, William, *Paddington Past and Present* (London, 1853)

Smiles, Samuel, *Brindley and the Early Engineers* (John Murray, 1874)

Smith, George, *Our Canal Population: A Cry from the Boat Cabins – With Remedy* (London, 1879)

White, William, *History, Gazetteer and Directory of Nottinghamshire* (Sheffield, 1832)

White, William, *History, Directory and Gazetteer of Staffordshire* (Sheffield, 1834)

Manuscript Sources

BCN Cottage Rent Journal (Midsummer and Lady Day) TNA RAIL 810/487

Birmingham Canal Navigations (BCN) Gauge Register 1925 TWA GD BW165/7/4/42

canal-boat inspector's pocket book CRO LUNo3897/7

canal-boat registers CRO LUR/57/5, CRO LUN 4452/1

declaration note TWA EP D1954

Grand Junction Canal boat (gauge) register 1818 TNA RAIL 830/56

Harecastle tunnel log book TWA EP D7074

Martin, Florence M., 'Elementary Education in the Poor Law Union of Runcorn from 1870–1903', M.Ed. thesis, University of Durham (1970), CRO 2401

North Staffordshire Railway Co. Canals Dept Wages Ledger 1850–1930 TWA EP 20001.146

Copies of the *Northwich Guardian* are kept at Northwich Library

Pickford's miscellaneous books and letters for 1818–1865 TNA RAIL 1133/149

register of boats CRO QDN4/1

Shropshire Union Railway and Canal Co. Staff Register for 1862–1897 TNA RAIL 623/67

toll ticket TWA EP D7619

wage books CRO D1361/1-3

Modern Works

Atkinson, Glen, *The Canal Duke's Collieries* (2nd edn, Neil Richardson, 1998)

Bagwell, Philip S., *The Transport Revolution* (Routledge, 1974)

Bennett, W., 'Welfare of Canal Boat Children', *Perspectives in Public Health*, May 1955, vol. 75 no. 5, 328–331

Boughey, Joseph and Hadfield, Charles, *British Canals: The Standard History* (Tempus Publishing, 2008)

Bowen, Paul, 'English canal-boat children and the education issue 1900–1940: towards a concept of traveller education?', *History of Education*, 30: 4, 359–378 (2001)

Burton, Anthony, *The Great Days of the Canals* (David & Charles, 1989)

Burton, Anthony, *The Canal Builders* (Tempus Publishing, 2005)

Clarke, Mike, *The Leeds & Liverpool Canal* (Carnegie Press, 1990)

Cobb, H.S., 'Railway and Canal Records in the House of Lords Record Office', *Railway and Canal Historical Society Journal*, March 1998

Corrie, Euan, *Tales from the Old Inland Waterways* (David & Charles, 2005)

Crecraft, Pat, 'This Special Kind of Traffic', *Waterways Journal Vol. 9*

De Salis, Henry, *Bradshaw's Canals and Navigable Rivers of England and Wales* (David & Charles, 1969)

Evans, Kathleen M., *James Brindley: Canal Engineer* (Churnet Valley Books, 1997)

Faulkner, Alan, 'Fellows, Morton and Clayton', *NarrowBoat*, Spring 2007

Faulkner, Alan, 'Fellows, Morton and Clayton', *NarrowBoat*, Summer 2007

Freer, Wendy, *Women and Children of the Cut* (Railway and Canal Historical Society, 1995)

Freer, Wendy and Foster, Gill, *Canal Boatmen's Missions* (Railway and Canal Historical Society, 2004)

Gregg, Pauline, *A Social and Economic History of Britain, 1760–1970* (6th edn, G. Harrap & Co. Ltd, 1971)

Hadfield, Charles, *British Canals: An Illustrated History* (Phoenix House, 1959)

Hadfield, Charles, *The Canal Age* (David & Charles, 1968)

Hadfield, Charles, 'An Approach to Canal Research', *Railway and Canal Historical Society Journal*, March 1998

Hadfield, Charles and Biddle, Gordon, *Canals of North-West England, Vols I and II* (David & Charles, 1970)

Hanson, Harry, *The Canal Boat-Men 1760–1914* (Manchester University Press, 1975)

Hanson, Harry, *Canal People* (David & Charles, 1978)

Higgs, Edward, *A Clearer Sense of the Census* (HMSO, 1996)

Hope, Edward William, *Health at the Gateway: Problems and International Obligations of a Seaport City* (Cambridge University Press, 1931)

Howat, Irene and Nicholls, John, *Streets Paved with Gold: The Story of the London City Mission* (Christian Focus Publications Ltd, 2003)

Jones, Christopher M., 'Canal Boat Registers', *NarrowBoat*, Spring 2007

Knowles, L.C.A., *Industrial and Commercial Revolutions* (George Routledge & Sons, 1937)

Macleod, Roy M., 'Social Policy and the Floating Population', *Past and Present*, 35 (1966), 101–132

Maxwell, Ian, *Your Irish Ancestors: A Guide for the Family Historian* (Pen & Sword, 2008)

Owen, David, *Canals to Manchester* (Manchester University Press, 1977)

Paget-Tomlinson, Edward, *Illustrated History of Canal & River Navigations* (Landmark Publishing, 1993)

Perrott, David (ed.), *The Ordnance Survey Guide to the Waterways: North* (Robert Nicholson Publications Ltd, 1985)

Perrott, David (ed.), *The Ordnance Survey Guide to the Waterways: Central* (Robert Nicholson Publications Ltd, 1987)

Perrott, David (ed.), *The Ordnance Survey Guide to the Waterways: South* (Robert Nicholson Publications Ltd, 1987)

Pyper, John, 'Last Traffics', *NarrowBoat*, Spring 2009

Ransom, P.J.G., *The Archaeology of Canals* (World's Work Ltd, 1979)

Rigby, Janet, *Life on the Lancaster Canal* (Landy Publishing, 2006)

Rolt, L.T.C., *Navigable Waterways* (Longman, 1971)

Rolt, L.T.C., *Narrow Boat* (History Press, 2009)

Rose, Lionel, *The Erosion of Childhood: Child Oppression in Britain 1860–91* (Routledge, 1991)

Shill, Ray, 'Gauging Boats on the BCN', *NarrowBoat*, Spring 2007

Sillitoe, Paul, 'Early Boat Registers', *NarrowBoat*, Spring 2009

Stammers, Michael, *Mersey Flats and Flatmen* (National Museums and Galleries on Merseyside, 1993)

Sullivan, Dick, *Navvyman* (Coracle, 1983)

Taylor, Mike, 'Tom Puddings in the 1960s', *Waterways Journal Vol. 9* (Boat Museum Society, 2007)

Wilkes, Sue, *Narrow Windows, Narrow Lives* (History Press, 2008)

Wilkes, Sue, *Regency Cheshire* (Robert Hale, 2009)

Online Sources

'Ealing and Brentford: Education', *A History of the County of Middlesex: Volume 7: Acton, Chiswick, Ealing and Brentford, West Twyford, Willesden* (1982), 162–170; http://www.british-history.ac.uk/report.aspx?compid=22588

Freer, Wendy, 'Canal Boat People 1840–1970', e-thesis, University of Nottingham (1991); http://etheses.nottingham.ac.uk

Matthews, Mark D., 'Shipping and local enterprise in the early eighteenth century', *Journal of Transport History* 24/2 (n.d.); manchesteruniversity press.co.uk

'Paddington: Protestant Nonconformity', *A History of the County of Middlesex: Volume 9: Hampstead, Paddington* (1989), 260–264; www.british-history.ac.uk/report.aspx?compid=22676

'Religious History: Protestant Nonconformity', *A History of the County of Warwick: Volume 7: The City of Birmingham* (1964), 411–434; www.british-history.ac.uk/report.aspx?compid=22980

Abbreviations

CRO	Chester Record Office
TNA	The National Archives
TWA EP	The Waterways Archive, Ellesmere Port
TWA GD	The Waterways Archive, Gloucester Docks

INDEX

trade unions, 91, 98, 132–133
tramroads, 16, 76, 113, 148
Trent, 5, 25, 74, 80, 101, 127, 134, 139, 147, 154, 163, 167
Trent & Mersey Canal, 5–7, 10, 13–17 *passim*, 19, 25, 31, 32, 46, 53, 54, 71, 77, 102, 123, 129, 139, 147, 163, 187
trows, 21, 148
tunnels, 14, 15, 40, 45, 53, 72, 75, 128, 162, 186

Union Canal, 139, 169, 188
Uxbridge, 149, 163

Virtual Waterways Archive Catalogue, 33, 35, 36, 128, 131, 134, 164

wages, 11, 22, 38, 90, 74, 76, 81, 85, 93, 97, 98, 129, 130, 148, 150, 153, 155, 158, 160–163 *passim*, 167, 169
Wain, James, 19
Wakefield family, 18–19, 95
Wales, 99, 100, 102, 104–106 *passim*, 108, 114, 115, 160–161, 164, 174
Walsall, 157
wars, 18, 30–32 *passim*, 45, 85, 97–98, 99, 100, 105, 114, 137

Warwickshire, 34, 131, 157, 175, 177, 179, 185
watchmen, 41, 81, 130
Waterman's Hall, 29, 31, 127, 129
watermen, 29, 42, 44, 98, 108, 112, 113, 131, 133, 165, 178, 179
waterways archives, 33, 35, 36, 44, 67, 84, 125, 127, 128, 131, 162–164, 170
Weaver, 3, 17, 21, 46, 95, 101, 113, 127, 129, 134, 138, 145, 158, 162, 164, 187
Wedgwood, Josiah, 5–7 *passim*, 25, 168
West Drayton, 93, 95
Wey, 3, 156
wharfinger, 31, 42, 75, 113, 144
wherries, 21, 66
Wigan Coal & Iron Co., 24
wills, 33, 106, 114, 133, 141, 142, 160, 170–174 *passim*
Wilts & Berks Canal, 144, 159
Wolverhampton, 38, 42, 85, 94, 126, 128, 159–160, 177
Worcester(shire), 25, 26, 39, 51, 59, 109, 112, 139, 175
Worcester and Birmingham Canal, 139